Beginner's Guide to Bird Watching

Little Owl, taken from a hide at night, with flash-bulb

Beginner's Guide to Bird Watching

REG HARRISON

Pelham Books - London

First published in Great Britain by Pelham Books Ltd
52 Bedford Square, London WC1B 3EF
1974

ISBN 0 7207 0747 1

Set and printed in Great Britain by
Tonbridge Printers Ltd, Peach Hall Works, Tonbridge, Kent
in Baskerville eleven on thirteen point on paper supplied by
P. F. Bingham Ltd, and bound by James Burn
at Esher, Surrey

Contents

List of Illustrations

Half-tone illustrations

Frontispiece : Little Owl

Between pages 80 and 81

Diagrams and figures

All photographs and drawings are by the author

Acknowledgements

The author is grateful to the following for information and help in compiling 'another bird book':

The Editors of *British Birds* magazine, and particularly James Ferguson-Lees, for permission to reproduce in the Preface the model 'code' for bird note-taking.

The Royal Society for the Protection of Birds for providing numerous pamphlets and leaflets which it publishes, especially the booklet *Wild Birds and the Law*.

The British Trust for Ornithology for permission to reproduce 'how to make a nest box from one piece of wood' from its pamphlet on *Nest Boxes*, and information regarding its various publications and leaflets.

The author could have submitted this manuscript to a dozen personally known and experienced bird watchers, and would have had a dozen entirely differing views and comments. He has refrained from doing so, and takes entire responsibility for the work, based on hard-won experience and knowledge.

Why this book?

This is not 'just another bird book'. There are dozens of bird books and field guides, several on bird watching alone (most of the latter are now out-of-print), and they confuse the beginner by starting off with the whole British List – some 426 species, scientific names and all. If the persistent bird watcher sees more than half of these in a lifetime he is lucky!

This work is aimed at the thousands who take up bird watching every year for the first time, whether they be boys or girls, adults who want a rewarding and satisfying spare-time hobby, or retired people looking for an absorbing yet comparatively inexpensive way of spending increased leisure all the year round. The field guides, excellent though they are, overwhelm the beginner with over 500 species – in the European books there are nine woodpeckers as against only three in England and none in Ireland; twelve tits, scores of sandpipers and other difficult waders, many of them hardly ever likely to turn up in these islands, let alone be recognised by the casual watcher.

So why not concentrate on the birds one is *likely* to find? That cuts us down to about 230 species – birds you can expect to find and recognise by sight and sound after a little experience. Then, having referred to your field guide or home-based book for further information, more detail and a coloured figure, you have a basis on which to proceed further.

You can then add more warblers or woodpeckers or waders, but you will already have got a grounding in the basic families and species, and can now put your birds into their correct category or family, which you could hardly expect to do if you had attempted to swallow a comprehensive field guide at the start!

It is too often assumed that one has only to buy a reliable 'bird book' with coloured plates, see an unfamiliar species, whizz through the pages and say 'that's it' in a few minutes. That is done hundreds of times, and the bird 'recognised' in the book is more often than not one that has occurred here perhaps once in fifty or a hundred years! 'But,' says the indignant reader, 'I'm sure of it!' It might be, once in a thousand instances.

Ask an experienced ornithologist, perhaps a member of your local bird club, and he will begin to express doubts, ask for very much more detail, and probably pour cold water on your record. How often has the oft-reported golden oriole turned out to be, on sober investigation, a green woodpecker flying under the woodland trees in dappled sunlight! Yes, 'golden' it may have seemed – the British Rarities Committee has too often borne this out.

The author had such an experience as a mere schoolboy, and more recently was able to prove to a field study group how easy it would be to run away with such unlikely conclusions after a hasty sighting. And this will apply to other rarities and vagrants, too. Purple heron, honey buzzard, several rare and difficult sandpipers, many scarce warblers, pipits and buntings, which often puzzle the most experienced watchers, all have their sighters, who are of course quite disappointed when their records are turned down by the ornithologists. Possibly the time of year was unlikely, the habitat wrong, the plumage in doubt, wind and weather just not right to bring such a visitor in. Unless the evidence is convincing and there is some corroboration from one or more competent and reliable observers, then the record is most likely to be rejected.

Doubting Thomases these people may seem, but vague and incomplete observations from those who are far from being experienced watchers would, if accepted, only make official records unreliable and misleading. That is why we find in the bird reports many species are 'square-bracketed', i.e. : [Water Pipit] which means, not that there is any doubt of the watcher's veracity, but of the unquestioned identification of the species.

The author has had reported to him 'a golden eagle with a six-foot wing span' which on investigation turned out to be a common buzzard with a three-foot wing span! Also a 'Nightingale' singing at night in a most unusual spot in a built-up area. It turned out to be a robin singing when the street lighting was switched on! It is remarkable how few people seem to be able to describe accurately either size, colour, wing pattern or calls of a bird, often days or weeks after they have seen the bird! Hence the importance of an admirable code drawn up by the magazine *British Birds* in 1952. Here it is :

With the great spread of bird watching in recent years, records are now being submitted by observers of widely varying ability and experience . . . The verification of sight-records is becoming increasingly difficult . . . Rejection of a record should not be taken to imply that we regard identification as wrong; it may simply mean that insufficient proof has been provided . . . Do not record a bird as seen unless you have taken down on the spot its characteristics before consulting a book. It is entirely unsatisfactory to view a bird in the field, taking insufficient notes, and then, finding its supposed portrait or description in a book, even a short time afterwards, to proceed to work out an account or sketch of what was seen.

Field notes should state :

1. Distance of bird from you, whether you were using glasses or not, and nature and direction of light.

2. Nature of ground it was on and what other birds (if any) it was associating with.

3. Whether you saw it from different angles, whether at rest or in flight; whether from above or below. (The more varied the conditions of observation the better.)

4. What were its actions and what was the character of its flight compared with other birds.

5. Its general form as compared with other birds, and how it differed from other birds at all like it which are known to you.

6. Its size, provided it could be compared with that of another bird of a known species seen close to it. (Otherwise estimates of size are very unreliable.)

7. Particular points in structure as compared with other birds, such as size and shape of bill, length of legs and feet, shape of wing, length of tail.

8. Colour of bill, legs and feet; any distinctive white or colour patches or markings, and their exact position. (Some general anatomy should be learnt so that you can give the colour of wing-coverts, under tail-coverts, nape, throat, chin, or other parts of the plumage accurately.)

9. So far as possible, an exact description of the whole plumage of the bird, not only the parts that you think may help in identifying it.

10. Any calls or notes, indicating especially the quality of the sound (harsh, rattling, shrill, hoarse, liquid, etc.) and comparison with notes of other species if this assists the description.

This may at first seem a rather frightening task, but if it is approached in the right way, and appreciating the reasons why the information is asked for, then the beginner is far more likely to become a reliable observer whose word and work will be respected. This code could usefully be pasted in the front of every bird book taken into the field but you won't be able to make *complete* field notes every time!

The bird watcher should be one who enjoys the hobby for its healthy outdoor activities, for pleasure in colour and movement, delight in songs and calls, and the thrill of adding a new species to one's list. One can be a 'loner' or a member of a group – there is no hard and fast rule or code to follow.

Preface: Why this book?

In this book scientific terms are kept to a minimum; every worthwhile field guide gives you a diagram showing the correct description of the different parts of a bird – valuable in writing down your field descriptions. (See Note 8 above.) Later on you will familiarise yourself with the orders, families, races and sub-species listed in almost every bird book, whether for use in the field or at home. Concentrate on the birds chosen in this beginner's guide, and you will be better able to tackle further species and families as they occur.

Later on we shall discuss the difficulties and differences in the appearances of birds under varying conditions, in different seasons, and as compared with the orthodox coloured plates. We shall go through the simplified bird list – always in the same correct scientific order, however – for recognition by sight and sound. This should help the reader to become familiar with orders and families, so that any subsequent bird book will not only be easier and quicker to use, but less familiar birds can be added to one's lists and given their correct status.

Today, bird watchers can be numbered in hundreds of thousands, whereas in the author's early years there were probably only a few thousand, mostly unorganised and largely out of touch with each other. Then, too, the field guide was unknown; there were few bird clubs or ornithological societies. Binoculars were a rare luxury, and the author began his watching with a well-made little pocket telescope (costing one-and-ninepence!) and a copy of John's *British Birds in their Haunts*, which could not be taken into the field. Perhaps today the choice in both books and equipment is much too wide and varied – hence this book.

CHAPTER ONE

Why bird watching?

There is no doubt the study of all branches of wild life becomes more and more popular each year, and the growing interest in the protection and preservation of wild creatures, plants and trees, subject to increasing pressures of human 'progress' and pressures for living space, has created international concern for life that is threatened all over the world and even in the seas.

Of all branches of natural history – botany, geology, mycology, entomology, and many others – ornithology, bird watching to us, is unquestionably the most popular and rapidly growing pursuit of all. Not only has it much more literature in both book and journal form, but its presentation on film and television, especially in colour, has added a new dimension and introduced the subject to many who have hitherto given it but casual attention. Its devotees can now be counted in at least six figures; the membership of the Royal Society for the Protection of Birds has grown from a few thousands to over 130,000 at the time of writing this chapter, and the flourishing condition (47,000 members) of the Young Ornithologists' Club augurs well for the future of bird-watching in Britain.

There is no bar either of age, sex, occupation or experience in the bird world. Anyone can 'join', anyone can 'begin' – any time, anywhere. Even the housebound and disabled can enjoy bird watching at home, from indoors or in the garden. What a wealth of interest and knowledge can be created by a window-sill bird table, a nest box within view of the bedroom or sitting room, often with photographic and other possibilities. But a later chapter is devoted to this very subject, where it is dealt with exhaustively and adequately.

Bird watching takes us out into the open air and can be studied all the year round; there is no close season. The vitality of wild birds, their plumage – changing with the seasons – their songs and calls, nesting activities, migration, can be observed in any part of the country, from the wildest and bleakest landscape (where we often get the most attractive species, by the way) to the city parks and lakes. A friend of the author, an experienced ornithologist, lives on the outskirts of London and claims that it is one of the best bird watching areas in Britain!

Our lives would certainly be the poorer if there were no birds; indeed, many scientists claim that but for their activities we would be soon overwhelmed by the insect population which multiplies in many cases million-fold in a comparatively short time, plus all the creeping, crawling and burrowing pests that live in the earth and attack trees and crops. Birds, too, are vital barometers in the contemporary problems of pesticides and pollution. Their importance cannot be over-estimated, and one of the many purposes of present-day bird study is to investigate cause and effect, problem and solution, so that less toxic chemicals may be devised to protect not only the crops and save wild life, but our own lives as well.

Bird watching need therefore not be just another pleasant but purposeless pursuit. We have still to solve many mysteries of wild life, and although birds have been studied and much more has been written about them than of any other branch of natural history, there is still a vast amount of knowledge yet untapped. The British Trust for Ornithology, for instance, conducts regular enquiries into some phase of bird study, and this is where the amateur comes in and helps to provide the ornithologist with first-hand observations and records. There are still many gaps in individual county records, even of breeding species. Valuable information is furnished by the qualified bird-ringer – who was once just a beginner in bird watching!

It was, for instance, an Essex schoolboy who first made systematic observations on how the Jay buries acorns in autumn – and remembers where he has hidden them during the winter!

Who are the bird watchers? People from every walk of life can be found in the bird clubs, and there is scarcely a part of the British Isles that is not covered by an ornithological society. Crowned heads and coronets have found relaxation, cabinet ministers and other members of Parliament have sponsored bills for the welfare and protection of birds, and taken a practical interest in organisations concerned with protection and conservation.

Top executives, people with great responsibilities in commerce and industry, policemen, teachers, farmers, parsons, musicians, actors (and some very famous names indeed in these last two categories can be included), technicians and farm hands, all have found bird watching a relaxing and worthwhile pursuit. In fact, from school children to those who have spent a lifetime in pursuit of birds, there is no calling that does not include many bird watchers.

And that is a reminder – 'in pursuit of birds'. Just as the sincere bird photographer should have as his first consideration the welfare of the bird itself, so the conscientious watcher should at all times obey an as yet unwritten code of conduct.

Too often, when some rare and possibly tired migrant has dropped down somewhere in Britain to rest and recuperate from a long flight before continuing its journey, the grape-vine becomes alerted and bird enthusiasts from many parts of the country journey to see this vagrant which may have occurred for the first time this century. The creature is harassed, put up to see the markings and perhaps hear the call; ringers encircle it with a view to trapping it; photographers stalk it. There they are, all in a semi-circle round the unfortunate creature, dozens of pairs of binoculars and telescopes at the ready. Every hotel or pub in the vicinity is full of bird watchers; no wonder irate landowners complain of trespass, broken fences, gaps in hedges and damaged crops! Through the activities of a minority, bird watchers get a very poor reputation in many places.

In some places responsible local societies have kept quiet about casual rarities for the very reasons given above, and have even given out misleading information so that the bird 'chasers' themselves are deceived. Unless we can keep to a code of decency and avoid such occurrences, bird watchers as a whole will acquire a bad name. It has happened that where the general public has created disturbances and trespass in national parks and restricted areas, such places have been closed to everyone through the thoughtless actions of a few.

If you know or hear of places where rarities rest, or nest, contact your local society for confirmation and leave it at that. *If* you can see these birds without in the least disturbing them, well and good, but be guided by the conscientious and experienced watcher, and be concerned for the welfare of the bird. They have enough natural enemies without creating more!

To conclude this chapter, here are two more reasons why we should become bird watchers, from two well-known naturalists of the past, but whose work and writings are by no means forgotten.

The first is from *Wild Nature's Ways* by Richard and Cherry Kearton, (1903), pioneers in bird photography. It might be called sentimental today but it expresses the basic longing of a human being cooped up in a city, for the wide open spaces of his birth and youth :

Man is a creature of strange follies, and my heart goes out in feminine tenderness to the poor fellow who lost a situation and £300 a year because he could not resist the temptation to run away to his beloved native hills when, in fancy, he heard the grouse* becking whilst lying in his bed at dawn on the 12th August in a far-away, grimy manufacturing town.

*A typical call of the grouse moor is 'go-back, go-back'. The 'glorious twelfth' is of course the start of the grouse shooting season.

Secondly, Richard Jefferies (1848–87), whose books are now counted among the classics, wrote :

> It is enough to be on the grass in the shadow of green boughs, to listen to the songs of summer, to drink in the sunlight, the air, the flowers, the sky, the beauty of all; or among the hill-tops to watch the white clouds rising over curved hill-lines, their shadows descending the slope, or on the beach to listen to the sweet sigh as the smooth sea runs and recedes.

CHAPTER TWO

Equipment

Bird watchers are fortunate in their hobby in that it can be one of the cheapest of all : one can spend a minimum and make the most of it, as the bird watchers of, say fifty or sixty years ago had to do, or can lavish money on expensive equipment such as super binoculars and telescopes, top-price still and ciné cameras, tape recorders of the most versatile kind, and take birding holidays in any part of the world, including the Antarctic and the Galapagos Islands!

But will the latter people get any more real pleasure and interest out of their hobby that those with limited means? Often the harder one has to work for one's money and the greater the difficulties encountered – in this and any other leisure-time pursuit – the greater the rewards and appreciation.

Basically, all the beginner needs is a good pair of eyes – and ears – a notebook, pencil and a bird book. These simple requirements will last for years and can be added to as their owner becomes more proficient and ambitious, and maybe more affluent.

One other minor item that practically every bird watcher, and indeed every experienced ornithologist, carries around is a 'bird list', in handy pocket form, consisting of the English names of the birds in scientific order, with spaces for ticking off or dating new discoveries. Many watchers keep two lists going, an annual one so that one year's bag can be compared with another, and a 'life list', a permanent one that is often the subject of good-natured boasting between amateurs. Such a list can be obtained from the British Trust for Ornithology, Beech Grove, Tring, Hertfordshire, for a few pence. Peterson's *Field Guide to the Birds of Britain and Europe* actually includes a bird list ready for ticking!

The most important next step, and probably the biggest of all for everyone, is the acquisition of a pair of binoculars, adding enormously to the pleasures of bird watching. Such a step is not to be lightly taken, as, with careful choice, these should last a lifetime and create no regrets. Don't run away with the idea that high-powered and expensive binoculars are necessarily the best for the purpose. The cost may be anything from ten or twelve pounds (the absolute minimum in these days) up to a hundred pounds or more. A high-pressure salesman may try to convince you that the higher the power – and the price – the better they are for bird watching. Far from it, and he has probably never watched a bird in his life!

There are good reasons why a standard pair of, say, 8 x 30 or 8 x 40 binoculars suits most people, but these figures need a little explaining. The first – 8 – is the magnification of the eye-piece, and anything from 7 to 9 or 10 is normal and the most popular even with the watcher of long experience. The second figure – 30 or 40 or 50 (or more) is the size of the other end of the glasses, in millimetres. It is a good rule that if the first figures goes into the second figure more than three times, then the binocular is satisfactory, other things being equal, for bird watching.

A glass of 10 x 50 gives a high magnification and a wide field of view, but there is a snag here. High magnification usually means a heavier instrument, thus it is not always possible to use these without a tripod or other firm support, and the range is comparatively smaller. A 20 x 50 binocular sounds most attractive to the beginner, but unless he is prepared to hump around an equally heavy tripod or rely on car-top or other support for his 'bargain', disappointment is likely to result.

For birds on the sea or across wide stretches of water, there is something to be said for these high-powered glasses, but it is more difficult to pick up moving objects with them, and in any case the modern telescope, described briefly later on, will answer most of the problems that a reasonable pair of standard binoculars will not solve.

There is a very wide choice of make and design on the market today; the dealers that advertise regularly in the 'bird' magazines can be relied upon to give satisfaction, and an 8 x 30 or 8 x 40, or for a wider field a 7 x 50, can be recommended. The visual comparison through the human eye will not reveal a great deal of difference between these three sizes. Anything less than 7x – there used to be some very good 6x binoculars on the market – have now been superseded by somewhat higher magnifications.

To test and adjust a pair of binoculars for the first time, look through the eye pieces and bend the centre bar until you see a complete circle – not two circles overlapping. Then focus on an object about 20 ft. or 25 ft. away – say a chimney stack or a tree-top in full leaf – close the right eye and check whether the detail seen on the distant object is crystal-clear. This is done by using the centre screw. Now, closing the left eye, check whether the object is as clear with the right as it was with the left eye. If it is not so, turn the adjustable ring on the right eyepiece, either to left or right, until the result is as good as it was with the other eye. Now look at the figures engraved on the rim. They may read zero, *plus* 1 or 2, or *minus* 1 or 2, but whatever they read when you are satisfied that *both* eyepieces reveal a clear picture, that is the optimum for your sight at any distance and should not need to be adjusted again.

If, however, you lend your instrument to anyone else they *may* have to alter this adjustment to suit their own eyesight, so always remember what the correct reading is for your own individual sight, and re-adjust the glasses afterwards. Using only the central screw your glasses should now give you clear vision at any required distance. Many binoculars will only focus down to about 16 ft. or so, but this is usually no drawback.

There are older types of binoculars which have both eye-pieces adjustable, and there was usually no centre-screw, but these are time-wasting instruments from the bird watcher's point of view, as by the time correct focus has been secured, the bird has usually gone!

Another big advance in the modern glass is the 'bloomed' lens, coated either with a purplish or straw-coloured pigment which does not however, affect the true colours seen through the lenses. This treatment increases the light-gathering properties and enables us to see much more clearly the details of plumage in very poor light as at dusk, or in dull weather and misty conditions.

One final tip : *always* carry your binoculars slung round your neck, either within the case provided or 'at the ready'. This is not mere ostentation but sound commonsense. If you get into the bad habit of carrying your glasses in your hand, you may stumble – and bird watchers are familiar with the roughest of rough ground! – and the first thing that goes is a good pair of binoculars, which may need expensive repairs if nothing worse. Remember the prisms through which you obtain your views are very delicately adjusted indeed, and will not stand rough treatment. A useful accessory is a rubber cap for the eyepieces, to keep the wet out, or one can easily be made from a strip or two of plastic material. This can be attached to the lanyard so that it is quickly removed for instant viewing.

The British Trust for Ornithology publishes an excellent guide to the choice of binoculars, and several makers issue useful pamphlets on the subject. Second-hand instruments can often be purchased at a reasonable price, but do test them thoroughly before buying, or ask the opinion of an experienced friend. Binoculars that appear 'battered' or have their covers peeling are best left alone. Some may appear 'loose-jointed', and only the expert repairer could say whether they can be successfully adjusted.

The older types of Galilean field glasses (with 'straight-through' vision instead of reflective prisms) are of very little use to the bird watcher, nor are the opera glasses so-called, as their magnification is probably no more than 2x or 3x. Many people with the sight of only one eye use a monocular, and this is just as good as the 'twinned' binocular in every way, save that it does not give three-dimensioned viewing.

Much the same principles described above apply to telescopes, of which again there is a bewildering array on the market. They now have bloomed lenses, too, and are very valuable for watching across water and on the coast, but here too, the greater the magnification the smaller the field of view, and it is useless to expect to be able to pick up moving birds with a telescope. Used with a tripod, or rested on a car-top or against the trunk of a tree to hold it steady, it can be a valuable aid to the experienced watcher, but is not absolutely essential to the beginner.

Much can be learnt from within a 'hide', or 'blind' as our American friends call it, whether one intends to use photography or not. The innermost secrets of bird life are revealed to the concealed watcher, particularly in the breeding season, and notebook, camera and of course binoculars, with possibly a portable folding stool, will yield to the patient and painstaking many glimpses otherwise unobtainable.

Basically the hide is merely a canvas- or hessian-covered frame easily taken to pieces for transportation, which hides the observer from his 'victim'. In the early days of Oliver Pike and the Kearton Brothers (the late nineteenth and early twentieth centuries) it was considered vital to camouflage oneself completely, and much ingenuity and money was spent achieving this – a 'stuffed' cow, in the hollow body of which the photographer could sit and use his camera through a hole in front of the animal's chest; a sheep similarly treated so that the camera was completely hidden and operated at some distance with a 'remote control', usually a pneumatic tube and bulb very similar to the ones obtainable today. Hollow tree-trunks were used, hessian painted to look like a ivy-covered tree and stretched on wire netting; imitation rocks for shore work; and there were many others.

Through experience it was gradually learnt that the only need was to conceal the human silhouette – the bird did not care whether the hide was 'almost natural' or not. Today a mere 'cube' is sufficient, and there are several commercial hides available that can be erected and taken down with the minimum of trouble. These are equipped with interior pockets for films, notebooks and other assets – not forgetting sandwiches if the wait is to be prolonged! But more will be said in the chapter on bird photography about the technique of using a hide.

It goes without saying that the watcher or photographer should be suitably clad for the task. Waterproof clothing, or at least a lightweight nylon mac which can be packed away in a haversack or even in the pocket, is an essential. So too, is sober headgear. Nothing will put birds up more effectively than a bright-coloured tam-o'-shanter bobbing up and down behind a hedge or reeds, and a thatch of white hair needs covering, too! The surplus gear sold in army and navy stores is excellent for bird watching purposes, and an old haversack to carry the odds and ends is sufficient for most ornithological needs.

Good footwear is of course essential, waterproof boots being perhaps the best, but climbing and other types that are made to stand up to rough wear are just as useful. Marshes, fens, the vicinity of lakes and meres, and moorland bogs call for gumboots, but a day spent plodding over rough ground in them can be very exhausting.

One's movements, too, must be circumspect, slow and silent. It's no use whipping up glasses to the eyes and bobbing up behind a clump of reeds with sudden movements. Every experienced watcher knows the disappointment when some noise or movement from the edge of a stretch of desolate country puts up the wary redshank – rightly called 'the warden of the marshes' – and up goes every other bird, too, including the wanderer one has journeyed perhaps far to see! A morning's or even a day's bird watching can be ruined by haste and thought-lessness.

It is debatable whether to carry your field guide with you on expeditions of any kind. The newer soft-covered books may stand more knocking around than the hardbacks, but none of them will long survive howling gales, heavy rain and stinging sleet! Best thing is to keep it in the car, to consult after you have made the necessary field notes (see the Preface) and maybe sketched the characteristic features of the unknown species. Many experts leave all their books at home!

One last point. See that all your equipment – binoculars, telescope, camera, tape recorder and their accessories – is insured. It costs very little and may save the owner much anxiety and regret when some favourite piece of equipment goes for a burton! Any insurance office will quote for 'all risks' cover as is needed – loss, theft, etc. – and the resultant peace of mind is well worth the comparatively small annual sums involved. The author once had a practically new tape recorder and a valuable lens stolen from his locked car. Fortunately both were covered by insurance. Keep your car locked – and don't advertise the fact that you have left valuable apparatus inside!

In addition to the equipment mentioned in this chapter, the following additions are invaluable :

Once-inch Ordnance Survey maps of your own and other districts.
Field List of British Birds: Complete list 5p each; 25p for 6; short list 25p per dozen.
Binoculars, telescopes and cameras: J. M. Flegg 30p.
These publications are obtainable from the British Trust for Ornithology, Beech Lodge, Tring, Hertfordshire.

CHAPTER THREE

The British Bird List

We need not go deeply into the whys and wherefores of the British systematic check-list of 426 wild birds, but it is useful to keep in mind their sequence and purposes. One is often asked: what is the use of all this scientific jargon? There are sound reasons why every species – and this applies equally to flora, fungi, algae (seaweeds), lepidoptera (butterflies and moths), coleoptera (beetles), geology (fossils) and every other branch of natural history – should have a definite order, family and species grouping. This is based on the great work of Linnaeus, the Swedish naturalist, and many others.

In Linnaeus's system, universally adopted, every creature or plant (including man himself – *homo sapiens*) – has two Latin or scientific names – a generic one and a specific one. The first puts the species in a defined group, while the second names the actual species. All this may seem elementary to the modern student who goes in for biology, but it is necessary that the general reader should also appreciate the reasons for scientific classification. For instance, our common chaffinch is classed as *fringilla coelebs* – the generic name denoting the finches group, and the second the actual species name, which in this case means 'bachelor', given because of the characteristic splitting up of the sexes in winter, males and females usually going into separate flocks.

Similarly the common wren is *troglodytes troglodytes* – the first meaning the wren group, and the second the correct name of the species which, in this case, as in many others, coincide, giving us the typical species in the group. There are, however, in this case other races, the St Kilda wren being *troglodytes troglodytes hirtensis,* thus distinguishing it from the typical wren. The generic and specific names in this case mean a 'cave dweller', which the wren is in remote and wilder places and certainly was in prehistoric times.

Such names are apt to be changed by scientists from time to time, however, but practically all modern bird books use this standard nomenclature known, since the last revision, as the Wetmore order, after an American scientific ornithologist. This giving of but one standard scientific name for each species is important. It is, first of all, internationally recognised, and can be understood equally by the French, Russian, or Swedish ornithologist – and those of every other country too, and the same applies in botany (where the experts seldom use the so-called 'English names because they are often confusing). When you think of the fact that large numbers of British birds have different names in different parts of the country – chaffinch, piefinch, spink, are all the same bird; so, too, are nightjar, fern owl, churn owl, goatsucker.

But the ordinary bird watcher need not conclude that it is necessary to learn these Latin or scientific names. Familiarity will come later, but it is still useful to know that *sterna* embraces all the tern family and that charadrius denotes a bird of the true plover family. Your field guide will give you these terms, and you will notice that in all the bird books and journals, these scientific names are in *italic*.

The British List is published by the British Ornithologists' Union, the senior scientific body in this country, but as you read in the preface, instead of burdening and confusing you with all these, we propose to describe, in the correct scientific order, however, some 230 of them as the most likely ones to be encountered in and around these islands. This course will also be followed in dealing with recognition by sight and sound, so that you will become familiarised with the place each species occupies in the standard bird list.

The orders are also based on evolutionary principles, beginning with the divers, the least developed and most primitive type of bird in Britain, still living almost entirely on and in the water and only crawling with difficulty to the nearest bit of land for breeding purposes. The grebes follow, slightly more developed but still more or less primitive birds. The last bird on the list – and therefore the most highly developed – is the Sparrow, which is found all over the Northern Hemisphere and elsewhere, and is parasitic on man!

In the following lists – which are by no means meant to be learned off by heart – the family name is given first. This is followed by the different members of the family with their Latin name. The number against each name refers to the fuller descriptions and illustrations in chapter VI, The Birds. Finally, a simplified code is used to describe the status of each bird in Britain.

C   common, and a breeding bird

L   local – found only in certain districts

R   resident, and therefore a breeding bird

S   scarce, and rare at any time

SV   summer visitor, and a breeding bird

V   vagrant – only an irregular visitor

WV   winter visitor

DIVERS (*Gaviidae*)

1. Black-throated diver (*Gavia arctica*) R.S.
2. Great Northern diver (*Gavia immer*) WV.
3. Red-throated diver (*Gavia stellata*) R.L.S.

GREBES (*Podicipedidae*)

4. Great Crested grebe (*Podiceps cristatus*) R.C.
5. Red-necked grebe (*Podiceps grisegena*) WV.
6. Slavonian grebe (*Podiceps auritus*) R.
7. Black-necked grebe (*Podiceps caspicus*) R.S. Also a spring and autumn visitor.
8. Little grebe (*Podiceps ruficollis*) R.C.

PETRELS (*Hydrobatidae*)
9. Leach's petrel (*Oceanodromo leucorhoa*) R.L.
10. Storm petrel (*Hydrobates pelagicus*) R.L.

SHEARWATER (*Procellariidae*)
11. Manx shearwater (*Puffinus puffinus*) R.L.

FULMAR (*Procellariidae*)
12. Fulmar Petrel (*Fulmarus glacialis*) R.C.

GANNET (order *Pelecaniformes*)
13. Gannet (*Sula bassana*) R.C.

CORMORANTS (order *Pelecaniformes*)
14. Cormorant (*Phalacrocorax carbo*) R.C.
15. Shag (*Phalacrocorax aristotelis*) R.L.

HERON (*Ardeidae*)
16. Common heron (*Ardea cinerea*) R.C.

BITTERN (*Ardeidae*)
17. Bittern (*Botaurus stellaris*) R.L.S. sometimes WV.
    Note: There are no wild Storks, Egrets or Cranes in Britain, except as very irregular, and therefore rare, visitors. In many districts the Common Heron is called a 'crane'.

SPOONBILL (*Threskiornithidae*)
18. Spoonbill (*Platalea leucorodia*) S.V.

DUCKS (*Anatidae*)
19. Mallard (*Anas platyrhynchos*) R.C.WV.
20. Teal (*Anas crecca*) R.C.WV.
21. Garganey (*Anas querquedula*) SV.L.
22. Gadwall (*Anas strepera*) R.L.
23. Wigeon (*Anas penelope*) R.L. also WV. in large flocks.
24. Pintail (*Anus acuta*) R.S. but also regular WV.
25. Shoveler (*Spatula clypeata*) R.C. but also regular WV.
26. Scaup (*Aythya marila*) WV.
27. Tufted duck (*Aythya fuligula*) R.C.WV.
28. Pochard (*Aythya ferina*) R.L.WV.
29. Golden-eye (*Bucephala clangula*) WV.
30. Velvet Scoter (*Melanitta fusca*) WV.
31. Common Scoter (*Melanitta nigra*) R.L.

32. Eider duck (*Somateria mollissima*) R.L.
33. Red-breasted Merganser (*Mergus serrator*) R. spreading; also WV.
34. Goosander (*Mergus merganser*) R.WV.
35. Smew (*Mergus albellus*) WV.
36. Sheld-duck (*Tadorna tadorna*) R.C.
37. White-headed duck (*Oxyura leucocephala*) WV. and R.
38. Mandarin duck (*Aix galericulata*) L.

GEESE (*Anatidae*)

39. Grey Lag (*Anser anser*) R.S. in Scotland; also WV.
40. White-fronted goose (*Anser albifrons*) WV.
41. Bean goose (*Anser fabalis*) WV.
42. Pink-footed goose (*Anser brachyrhynchus*) WV.
43. Snow goose (*Anser hyperboreus*) WV.
44. Brent goose (*Branta bernicla*) WV.L.
45. Barnacle goose (*Branta leucopsis*) WV.L.
46. Canada goose (*Branta canadensis*) R.C.

SWANS (*Anatidae*)

47. Mute swan (*Cygnus olor*) R.C.
48. Whooper swan (*Cygnus cygnus*) WV.
49. Bewick's swan (*Cygnus bewickii*) WV.

EAGLES (*Accipitridae*)

50. Golden eagle (*Aquila chrysaetos*) R.S.
51. Common Buzzard (*Buteo buteo*) R.L.
52. Rough-legged Buzzard (*Buteo lagopus*) S.V.
53. Sparrow Hawk (*Accipiter nisus*) R., said to be C.
54. Goshawk (*Accipiter gentilis*) S.
55. Red Kite (*Milvus milvus*) R.L.
56. Marsh Harrier (*Circus aeruginosus*) L.S.
57. Hen Harrier (*Circus cyaneus*) L.S.
58. Montagu's Harrier (*Circus pygargus*) L.S.
    family *Pandionidae*
59. Osprey (*Pandion haliaetus*) S.V.
    family *Falconidae*
60. Hobby (*Falco subbuteo*) L.S.
61. Peregrine Falcon (*Falco peregrinus*) R.L.

62. Merlin (*Falco columbarius*) R.L.WV.
63. Kestrel (*Falco tinnunculus*) R.C.

GROUSE (*Tetraonidae*)

64. Red grouse (*Lagopus lagopus scoticus/hibernicus*) R., locally C.
65. Ptarmigan (*Lagopus mutus*) R.L. in Scotland only.
66. Black grouse (*Lyrurus tetrix*) R.L.
67. Capercaillie (*Tetrao urogallus*) R.L.

PARTRIDGES (*Phasianidae*)

68. Red-legged partridge (*Alectoris rufa*) R.C.
69. Partridge (*Perdix perdix*) R.C.
70. Quail (*Coturnix coturnix*) SV.L.
71. Common Pheasant (*Phasianus colchicus*) R.C.

RAILS (*Rallidae*)

72. Water rail (*Rallus aquaticus*) R.L.
73. Corncrake (*Crex crex*) SV.
74. Moorhen (*Gallinula chloropus*) C.
75. Coot (*Fulica atra*) C.

OYSTERCATCHER (*Haematopodidae*)

76. Oystercatcher (*Haematopus ostralegus*) R.C., also WV.

LAPWING (*Charadriidae*)

77. Lapwing (*Vanellus vanellus*) R.C., also WV. in large numbers.

PLOVERS (*Charadriidae*)

78. Ringed plover (*Charadrius hiaticula*) R.C.
79. Little Ringed plover (*Charadrius dubius*) SV.
80. Grey plover (*Pluvialis squatarola*) WV.
81. Golden plover (*Pluvialis apricaria*) R.L.
82. Dotterel (*Eudromias morinellus*) SV.S.

TURNSTONE(*Charadriidae*)

83. Turnstone (*Arenaria interpres*) WV.

SNIPE (*Charadriidae*)

84. Common snipe (*Gallinago gallinago*) R.C.
    Jack snipe (*Lymnocryptes minimus*) WV. (no illustration)

WOODCOCK (*Charadriidae*)
85. Woodcock (*Scolopax rusticola*) R.C., also WV.
CURLEWS (*Charadriidae*)
86. Curlew (*Numenius arquata*) R.C., also WV.
87. Whimbrel (*Numenius phaeopus*) SV.S. Scotland only.
GODWITS (*Charadriidae*)
88. Black-tailed godwit (*Limosa limosa*) SV.L.
89. Bar-tailed godwit (*Limosa lapponica*) WV.
SANDPIPERS (*Charadriidae*)
90. Green sandpiper (*Tringa ochropus*) WV.C.
91. Wood sandpiper (*Tringa glareola*) WV.L.
92. Common sandpiper (*Tringa hypoleucos*) SV.
93. Redshank (*Tringa totanus*) R.C.
94. Spotted Redshank (*Tringa erythropus*) WV., rather L.
95. Greenshank (*Tringa nebularia*) SV.L.
KNOTS, STINTS (*Charadriidae*)
96. Knot (*Calidris canutus*) WV.
97. Purple Sandpiper (*Calidris maritima*) WV.
98. Little stint (*Calidris minuta*) WV.
98a. Temminck's stint (*Calidris temminckii*) WV.
99. Dunlin (*Calidris alpina*) SV.L.
100. Curlew Sandpiper (*Calidris ferruginea*) WV.
101. Sanderling (*Calidris alba*) WV.
RUFF (*Charadriidae*)
102. Ruff (female : Reeve) (*Philomachus pugnax*) SV.
AVOCET (*Charadriidae*)
103. Avocet (*Recurvirostra avosetta*) SV.
PHALAROPES (*Charadriidae*)
104. Grey phalarope (*Phalaropus fulicarius*) S.
105. Red-necked phalarope (*Phalaropus lobatus*) SV., very L.S.
STONE CURLEW (*Burhinidae*)
106. Stone Curlew (*Burhinus oedicnemus*) SV.S.L.
SKUAS (*Stercorariidae*)
107. Arctic skua (*Stercorarius parasiticus*) SV.
108. Great skua (*Stercorarius skua*) SV.

109. Long-tailed skua (*Stercorarius longicaudus*) S.

GULLS (*Laridae*)

110. Great Black-backed gull (*Larus marinus*) R., and C. locally

111. Lesser Black-backed gull (*Larus fuscus*) SV., and C. locally.

112. Herring gull (*Larus argentatus*) R.C.WV.

113. Common gull (*Larus canus*) R., C. only Scotland.
Glaucous gull (*Larus hyperboreus*) WV. (no illustration)

114. Black-headed gull (*Larus ridibundus*) R.C., also WV.

KITTIWAKE (*Laridae*)

115. Kittiwake (*Rissa tridactyla*) S.V.

TERNS (*Laridae*)

116. Black tern (*Chlidonias niger*) V. (spring and autumn pass.)

117. Common tern (*sterna hirundo*) SV.

118. Arctic tern (*Sterna paradisaea*) SV.

119. Roseate tern (*sterna dougallii*) SV.S.

120. Little tern (*sterna albifrons*) SV.L.

121. Sandwich tern (*Sterna sandvicensis*) SV.

AUKS (*Alcidae*)

122. Razorbill (*Alca torda*) R.L.
Little auk (*Plautus alle*) WV. (no illustration)

123. Guillemot (*Uria aalge*) R.L.

124. Black Guillemot (*Cepphus grylle*) R.L.

125. Puffin (*Fratercula arctica*) R.L.

DOVES (*Columbidae*)

126. Stock dove (*Columba oenas*) C.

127. Rock dove (*Columba livia*) R.

128. Wood pigeon (*Columba palumbas*) R.C., also WV.

129. Collared dove (*Streptopelia decaocto*) R.C.

130. Turtle dove (*Steptopelia turtur*) SV.C.

CUCKOO (*Cuculidae*)

131. Cuckoo (*Cuculus canorus*) SV.C.

OWLS (*Tytonidae*)

132. Barn owl (*Tyto alba*) R.
     family *Strigidae*
133. Snowy owl (*Nyctea scandiaca*) R.S.L.
134. Little owl (*Athene noctua*) R.C.
135. Tawny owl (*Strix aluco*) R.C.
136. Long-eared owl (*Asio otus*) R.L.
137. Short-eared owl (*Asio flammeus*) R.WV.
NIGHTJAR (*Caprimulgidae*)
138. Nightjar (*Caprimulgus eropaeus*) SV.L.
SWIFT (*Apodidae*)
139. Common swift (*Apus apus*) SV.
KINGFISHER (*Alcedinidae*)
140. Kingfisher (*Alcedo atthis*) R.C.
HOOPOE (*Upupidae*)
141. Hoopoe (*Upupa epops*) SV.
WOODPECKERS (*Picidae*)
142. Green woodpecker (*Picus viridis*) R.C.
143. Pied woodpecker (*Dendrocopos major*) R.C.
144. Barred woodpecker (*Dendrocopos minor*) R.L.
WRYNECK (*Picidae*)
145. Wryneck (*Jynx torquilla*) SV.S.
LARKS (*Alaudidae*)
146. Wood lark (*Lullula arborea*) R.S.
147. Skylark (*Alauda arvensis*) R.C.WV.
148. Shore lark (*Eremophila alpestris*) WV.
SWALLOWS (*Hirundinidae*)
149. Swallow (*Hirundo rustica*) SV.C.
150. House Martin (*Delichon urbica*) SV.C.
151. Sand Martin (*Riparia riparia*) SV.C.
GOLDEN ORIOLE (*Oriolidae*)
152. Golden oriole (*Oriolus oriolus*) S.SV.
CROWS (*Corvidae*)
153. Raven (*Corvus corax*) R.
154. Carrion crow (*Corvus corone corone*) R.C.
155. Hooded crow (*Corvus corone cornix*) R.C.WV.
156. Rook (*Corvus frugilegus*) R.C.

157. Jackdaw (*Corvus monedula*) R.C.
158. Magpie (*Pica pica*) R.C.
159. Jay (*Garrulus glandarius*) R.C.

CHOUGH (*Corvidae*)

160. Chough (*Pyrrhocorax pyrrhocorax*) R.L.

TITMICE (*Paridae*)

161. Great tit (*Parus major*) R.C.
162. Blue tit (*Parus caeruleus*) R.C.
163. Coal tit (*Parus ater*) R.C.
164. Crested tit (*Parus cristatus*) R.L. (in Scotland only)
165. Marsh tit (*Parus palustris*) R.C.
166. Willow tit (*Parus montanus*) R.L.
167. Long-tailed tit (*Aegithalos caudatus*) R.C.
    family *Mauscicapidae*
168. Bearded tit (*Panurus biarmicus*) R.L.

NUTHATCH (*Paridae*)

169. (*Sitta europaea*) R.C.

TREE CREEPER (*Certhiidae*)

170. Tree creeper (*Certhia familiaris*) R.C.

WREN (*Troglodytidae*)

171. Common Wren (*Troglodytes troglodytes*) R.C.

DIPPER (*Cinclidae*)

172. Dipper (*Cinclus cinclus*) R.L.

THRUSHES (*Muscicapidae*)

173. Mistle thrush (*Turdus viscivorus*) R.C.
174. Fieldfare (*Turdus pilaris*) WV.
175. Song thrush (*Turdus philomelos*) R.C.
176. Redwing (*Turdus iliacus*) WV.
177. Ring Ouzel (*Turdus torquatus*) SV.L.
178. Blackbird (*Turdus merula*) R.C.

WHEATEAR (*Muscicapidae*)

179. Wheatear (*Oenanthe oenanthe*) SV.C.

STONECHATS (*Muscicapidae*)

180. Stonechat (*Saxicola torquata*) R., formerly C., now L.
181. Whinchat (*Saxicola rubetra*) SV.C.

REDSTARTS *(Muscicapidae)*

182. Redstart *(Phoenicurus phoenicurus)* SV.C.

183. Black redstart *(Phoenicurus ochruros)* L.

NIGHTINGALE *(Muscicapidae)*

184. Nightingale *(Luscinia megarhynchos)* SV.L.

ROBIN *(Muscicapidae)*

185. Robin *(Erithacus rubecula)* R.C.

WARBLERS *(Muscicapidae)*

186. Grasshopper warbler *(Locustella naevia)* SV.L.

187. Savi's warbler *(Locustella lusinioides)* SV.R.

188. Reed warbler *(Acrocephalus scirpaceus)* SV.C.

189. Marsh warbler *(Acrocephalus palustris)* SV.L.

190. Sedge warbler *(Acrocephalus schoenobaenus)* SV.C.

191. Blackcap *(Sylvia atricapilla)* SV.C.

192. Garden warbler *(Sylvia borin)* SV.C.

193. Whitethroat *(Sylvia communis)* SV.C.

194. Lesser Whitethroat *(Sylvia curruca)* SV.C.

195. Dartford warbler *(Sylvia undata)* R.S.

196. Willow warbler *(Phylloscopus trochilus)* SV.C.

197. Chiff-chaff *(Phylloscopus collybita)* SV.C.

198. Wood warbler *(Phylloscopus sibilatrix)* SV.C.

GOLDCRESTS *(Muscicapidae)*

199. Goldcrest *(Regulus regulus)* R.C. and WV.

200. Firecrest *(Regulus ignicapillus)* WV.S.

FLYCATCHERS *(muscicapidae)*

201. Spotted flycatcher *(Muscicapa striata)* SV.C.

202. Pied flycather *(Ficedula hypoleuca)* SV.L.

DUNNOCK *(Prunellidae)*

203. Hedge Sparrow *(Prunella modularis)* R.C.

PIPITS, WAGTAILS *(Motacillidae)*

204. Meadow pipit *(Anthus pratensis)* R.C., also WV.

205. Tree pipit *(Anthus trivialis)* SV.C.

206. Rock pipit *(Anthus spinoletta)* R.C.

207. Pied wagtail *(Motacilla alba yarrellii)* R.C.

208. Grey wagtail *(Motacilla cinerea)* R.C.

209. Yellow wagtail *(Motacilla flava)* SV.C.

There are several sub-races: Blue-headed, Grey-headed, Ashy-headed, etc.

WAXWING (*Bombycillidae*)

210. Waxwing (*Bombycilla garrulus*) WV.

SHRIKES (*Laniidae*)

211. Grey Grey shrike (*Lanius excubitor*) WV.

212. Red-backed shrike (*Lanius collurio*) SV.L.

STARLING (*Sturnidae*)

213. Starling (*Sturnus vulgaris*) R.C.WV.

FINCHES (*Fringillidae*)

214. Hawfinch (*Coccothraustes coccothraustes*) R.L.

215. Greenfinch (*Carduelis chloris*) R.C., also WV.

216. Goldfinch (*Carduelis carduelis*) R.C.

217. Siskin (*Carduelis spinus*) R.L., also WV.

218. Linnet (*Acanthis cannibina*) R.C., also WV.

219. Twite (*Acanthis flavirostris*) R.L.

220. Redpoll (*Acanthis flammea*) R., also WV.

221. Bullfinch (*Pyrrhula pyrrhula*) R.C.

222. Crossbill (*Loxia curvirostra*) R.L., also WV.

223. Chaffinch (*Fringilla coelebs*) R.C.

224. Brambling (*Fringilla montifringilla*) WV.

BUNTINGS (*Emberizidae*)

225. Yellow Hammer (*Emberiza aureola*) R.C.

226. Corn bunting (*Emberiza calandra*) R.L.

227. Cirl bunting (*Emberiza circuls*) R.L.

228. Reed bunting (*Emberiza schoeniclus*) R.C.

229. Snow bunting (*Plectrophenax nivalis*) R.L.

SPARROWS (*Ploceidae*)

230. House sparrow (*Passer domesticus*) R.C.

231. Tree sparrow (*Passer montanus*) R.L.

CHAPTER FOUR

Where to find birds

The study of the living bird can begin in your own garden and surroundings at any time of year. City parks and gardens, sewage works and derelict canals, seemingly desolate estuaries and mudflats – all these will produce their own species of bird, often where the hand of man has lain heavily on the countryside. The black redstart, a rare British breeding bird before 1939, started breeding increasingly in the bombed sites of London and elsewhere, and is now found in other built-up areas.

Under strict protection, such species as the osprey, avocet, bittern, ruff, black-tailed godwit, savi's warbler and many others have come back to nest here after, in many instances, an absence of a hundred years or more. Others, unfortunately, like the nightingale, red-backed shrike, wryneck, chough and Dartford warbler, are decreasing, and we cannot as yet be sure of the reasons in every case; maybe a general European decline, side-effects of man's making, or destruction of habitat. Out of the blue came the collared dove, which ornithologists have been watching spread from the Far East during this century until it has now reached the west coast of Ireland – where does it go from there? It is anticipated that the time is not far off when we may welcome the Syrian woodpecker. The firecrest is increasingly recorded.

All this means that our bird populations do not remain stationary over the country, and there is no reason why every bird watcher should not participate in the work of the national organisations which inaugurate censuses and enquiries. It is largely the amateur that forms the major proportion of the form-fillers and reporters. If it were not for the spare-time watcher the results of nation-wide investigations would not have such wide coverage. Then, too, ornithologists are internationally-minded; every country has its scientific organisation that keeps in touch with others, exchanges information and records, and checks movements and fluctuations.

There is no part of the country in which bird life cannot be found – sometimes quite unexpectedly. Industrial areas such as Teesmouth and Mersey, power station sites such as Dungeness or Wylfa – all have their regular species and often their rarities. The east coast of England is probably one of the best in Europe in spring and autumn migrations for rarities, especially when the winds are easterly or north-easterly. Birds which only breed beyond the Arctic circle pass down our eastern coast in particular – these are classed as passage migrants of course – and the ringing stations there regularly produce scarce and unusual species every season.

But wherever you live you can be sure that someone, at some time, has authentically recorded something unusual. Even in the Midlands, storm-blown and out-of-course birds of purely oceanic origin, like gannet, puffin, little auk and fork-tailed petrel, have either been found dead or picked up exhausted.

The mainstay of the bird watcher is, however, the so-called resident and breeding bird and the summer and winter visitor whose occurrence can be looked for with confidence year by year at the appropriate time. Even in our suburban gardens, with their blackbirds and song thrushes, sparrows and starlings, blue tits and robins, there are changes to be recorded. The blackbird – or even the robin – that was there in the spring and possibly nested, is not necessarily the same one that comes to the bird table in December. You may get waxwings; bramblings are almost certain in snowy spells, while even the skylark and water-hen may arrive to partake of the food thrown out.

The sewage farm has been mentioned; if you have one of

these in your area and can obtain permission from the local sanitary authority to visit it (bird watching clubs usually have blanket permits for such places) you will be surprised at the variety of the visitors – waders of every kind, including some of the rare sandpipers, ruffs, godwits and others. These places are rapidly being 'modernised' and losing many of their choice birds, but the migrants have to rest and feed somewhere, and their new haunts have to be sought out and watched.

Fallow fields full of waste grain and weed seeds are fruitful places for pipits, larks, finches and buntings. Woodland edges are always good for the spring arrivals, the sparrow hawk and jay, nuthatch and maybe woodpeckers. Where there are plenty of alder trees by the stream or lake side, watch out for flocks of redpolls and siskins – often associated – and many of the tit family. Mature conifer plantations with their ripe cones will attract flocks of crossbills, tearing open the cones for the seeds within. Occasionally we get an invasion of nutcrackers – birds very much like over-grown starlings in shape and markings, arriving when their natural food crop has failed as far away as Siberia, and spreading all over the country if the numbers are large enough. Wild geese from Greenland and Siberia visit Britain in winter, and have definite habitats in many parts of this country until the end of March sees them once more turning back to their northern breeding territories. They can often be heard flying over at night time in mid-winter.

These are a few of the 'local' spots where one can find birds all through the months of winter. Continued unsettled and cold weather will drive still more birds down from Scotland and Scandinavia, seeking shelter and available food that is denied them in more northern regions.

Winter, too, is the time when huge flocks of waders and other shore birds feed on the tidelines and attract large numbers of watchers. Such spots as Hilbre and Point of Air on the Dee estuary; Morecambe Bay with tens of thousands of Oyster-catchers and other birds; the Ouse Washes; the Severn estuary; Chichester harbour; the Solway and many others have their

43

regular quotas of godwits, knot (often in astonishingly large flocks), curlew, dunlin, sanderling, etc. It is by no means unusual to be able to see 200,000 knot or 100,000 oystercatchers in such places. Most local bird clubs organise outings to them, and there are at least twenty large estuaries around our coasts where spectacular flocks will be seen under the right tidal conditions.

But there is no need to despair if one is unable to join in these delectable expeditions, where the various species of bird can be identified in the company of those who have spent many years at it. Many people prefer to be 'lone' watchers rather than join the masses who nevertheless find great pleasure in sharing their experience and knowledge.

The rapid-running streams of the north and west of Britain will almost always provide dipper and grey wagtail in identical habitats, while in summer the ring ouzel also frequents similar sites but is less often evident. Mature deciduous woods almost anywhere will produce the great spotted or pied woodpecker, possibly its much larger relative the green species; almost always nuthatch and, if carefully looked and listened for, the tree creeper. Where there is plenty of bramble and dog-rose cover blackcap and garden warbler, whitethroat and other summer visitors will be found from April to August. The wood warbler, with its canary-yellow 'waistcoat', favours the hanging or sloping oak and beech woods, and its distinctive song calls attention to its presence in summer. In the lighter type of woodland – birch, hazel and scrub – the soothing summer calling of the turtle dove will be heard. Where there is a birch-and-bracken association and a good but low ground cover, look out for the nightjar, but you are most unlikely to see or hear it in the day-time. The grasshopper warbler will often be found in similar conditions and also in very young conifer plantations.

Lakes and meres, whether in parkland or in isolation, will yield Canada goose, great crested grebe and its tiny relative the dabchick or little grebe, and of course the ubiquitous coot with its white shield, and the less gregarious moorhen or waterhen with its distinct red shield and white patches on wings and tail. Mallard, our commonest duck, are certain to be present all the year round. Tufted duck are resident, and therefore breeding, in many places, and in the shallows an elegant heron may stand stock-still, waiting for the unwary eel, frog, small fish or even water-vole to come within range of its stabbing beak.

Winter is probably the best time to see the large flocks of various species of duck – wigeon, pochard, teal, pintail and many others, while large rafts of various species of gull may roost during the season in the centres of large sheets of water. In more northerly waters, those distinctive swans, the whooper (larger than the mute swan and with a straighter neck and yellow beak patches) and Bewick's, much smaller, come to winter from their bleak breeding country. On the fringes of the water, if there are *phragmites* reeds present, look out for the reed warbler in summer, as it uses these plants to sling its deeply cupped nest, while in East Anglia a similar site might be used by the bearded tit or reed pheasant, a very much rarer and more local bird.

On the seashore in summer, apart from the usual ringed plovers and oystercatchers which breed on suitable beaches, gulls of various species are everywhere. The fulmar petrel, once confined almost entirely to places like St Kilda, has now spread down both our western and eastern coasts and is colonising suitable cliffs for nesting sites. Its typical gliding motion with almost rigid wings distinguishes it from any of the gulls. On our western coasts particularly, razorbill, guillemot and puffin will nest in large numbers on suitable cliffs. Four species of terns, or sea swallows, nest colonially on suitable beaches and dunes, round our coasts.

In the highlands there are rarer birds – the ospreys of Loch Garten and other places; the crested tit of the primeval Rothiemurchus Scots pine forest; the noisy greenshank of the moorlands; the occasional sighting of a golden eagle; or a pair of black-throated divers or Slavonian grebes may reward the visitor. Black grouse and ptarmigan, sometimes a capercaillie, and up in the high Cairngorms the rare dotterel can be found, with sometimes a pair of breeding snow buntings.

On the islands round our shores – and Britain is peculiarly favoured in this respect – bird watching can be a delight and revelation. In most cases the birds show little or no fear of man (generations of persecution on the mainland have taught birds to be wary even of the silhouette of man!) and one can approach nesting birds within a few feet. Places like Skokholm, Skomer, Grassholm and Ramsey can be visited by arrangement with the societies that look after these bird reserves off the Pembrokeshire Coast.

On the delightful Farne Islands off the Northumberland coast, and owned by the National Trust, it is possible to make daily visits during the whole of the breeding season, to see razorbills, guillemots, shags, cormorants, kittiwakes, and various gulls nesting on the precipitous cliffs. Hundreds of pairs of eider ducks and thousands of Arctic terns nest on the ground. Farther north the Bass Rock may be visited for its gannet colony.

Inland and coastal bird reserves can also be visited, mostly by permit. Large numbers of them belong to the Royal Society for the Protection of Birds, whilst many of the Norfolk Broads belong to the oldest established trust in Britain, the Norfolk Naturalists' Trust. There are other reserves which can be visited, Scolt Head, Lundy and Brownsea Island among them.

In short, there is hardly any spot in the whole of the British Isles where one will draw a blank so far as birds are concerned. Often the most unattractive piece of land will yield something worthwhile. Even our conifer plantations, derided as they are by many people, have been responsible for the increase in such birds as goldcrest, crossbill, siskin, redpoll, blackcock and others.

This is but a brief outline of the possibilities of bird watching all over the country and at all seasons of the year. The beginner who has not yet tasted the pleasures touched on in this chapter has something thoroughly satisfying to look forward to.

CHAPTER FIVE

Recognition by sight

Sight recognition of birds logically begins with a bird book containing coloured plates. But how often do we see the birds 'perched' as shown in almost all the older works when seldom was any species shown in flight. Then, too, these books show often the male only, in full breeding plumage, with every feather detailed in colour. Are these pictures of birds as helpful to the beginner as they are intended to be?

A bird's plumage varies; males and females are often utterly unlike in colour, size and pattern; with many species such as the gulls it is three or more years before they assume the full adult plumage; the season of the year affects the appearance of such birds as the ducks and others when they go into 'eclipse' plumage; the environment, the nature of the light falling on them, influence the colours we see. In short, when do we see true colour as depicted in the bird plates? Frequently all we see of a bird is a *silhouette*, either against the sky or perched in a tree. Thus, at any time of year, a shape and pattern may be far more useful to us than the possible presence of a red spot or a rather indistinct wing-bar. Colour must certainly enter into our final diagnosis, but even the most expensive bird books are of little help under poor or difficult conditions.

SHAPE AND SIZE

If the size and shape of a bird can be used to put it into a category or family to begin with, then identification becomes

47

easier and we need not yet consult a book. Take the case of an owl silhouetted against the sky at dusk or even in darkness. We don't have to see its plumage pattern or facial disc to know that it's an owl. Shape alone tells us that, and size will tell even the beginner whether it is a little owl (our smallest owl) or a tawny owl – the two most likely species – or the slimmer, whiter (if you can see that!) barn owl. It is unlikely to be the long-eared owl unless you are in or close to coniferous woods, and the only remaining species, the short-eared owl, is an inhabitant of open moorlands. Without our books, therefore, we have recognised an OWL, even without hearing it call – another clue which is dealt with in a subsequent chapter.

Similarly, we all know the shape of a duck, whether on water or dry land, or a woodpecker or a wood pigeon; these have distinctive shapes – and sizes – and we are on the way to putting our birds into categories or families, which narrows down the actual species we may be looking for. You will find, early in your bird watching, that almost all birds conform to 'family' shapes – tits, finches, warblers, waders, birds of prey, gulls, terns and so on, and combining this pattern with size we are on the way to recognise many species or at least put them into some group or other. We can also use this, as some people do, in a 'negative' way – it's *not* an owl, or a duck, a finch or a crow. So up to this point you have not consulted any book – and the illustrations in this chapter will, it is hoped, help considerably.

POSTURE

Having got a clear picture of identification with a minimum of detail, we can now add a third category – posture or attitude. This is the way in which a bird habitually 'poses' – its stance, which will in most cases be typical of that particular species or group. Thus, woodpeckers, with nuthatch and tree-creeper, are most often seen upright on tree trunks, climbing upwards (but the nuthatch can also climb downwards, and the tree-creeper often makes a spiral climb). Ducks are usually seen on water or in flight, but on land they have a very upright carriage, the legs being placed far back on the body. Birds of prey are usually to be seen in the air, often soaring (Buzzard), hovering (buzzard and kestrel). Tits are, more often than not, restless creatures, hardly ever still, often perching upside-down, using typical 'family' calls at the same time. So, too, are redpoll siskin and the goldcrest. Warblers are much the same in size and shape – the family resemblance – but they differ in other characteristics, and *all* of them have the typical, thin soft bill of the insectivorous birds (like robin, wren, dunnock), differing from the shorter, thicker seed-eating beak of the sparrows and all the finches.

In fact, a bird's beak is a sure indication of the way in which it earns its living. Look at the long, stabbing beaks of the fishermen – heron, gannet, kingfisher; the long, often curved, probing beaks of curlew, snipe, woodcock, godwit and other waders, each one distinctive and purpose-built to enable the species to earn its living in a specialised way, quite different from the pick-axe beaks of the crow family – all-purpose tools for omnivorous feeding. The flesh-tearing hooked beaks of the owls and the birds of prey, together with their curved talons, tell us their story at once.

FLIGHT

Flight is somewhat more difficult, but in very many instances we can with a little practice, identify a bird in the air without any other means, even if it is only a silhouette. Even at some distance it is often possible to recognise many a bird in flight by shape alone, or at least put it into a definite category – crow, gull, hawk, duck. Flight, too, has characteristics in families – the undulating flight of the woodpeckers (incidentally most woodland birds have comparatively short wing lengths to enable them to fly swiftly in and out of branches and trunks), the jerky flight of tits and other small birds; the purposeful straight flights of the crow family (as the crow flies is perfectly true), the characteristic skein flights of ducks, geese, gulls and many waders are all things to be learnt.

There are birds that fly very low over the ocean – shear-waters, correctly named; the merlin flies low over its moorland haunts. But if we study flight at all, we shall in a short time recognise the distinctive patterns of many species and the typical family resemblances. Flight alone is often valuable in itself, for recognition.

BEHAVIOUR

Another facet of sight identification is behaviour – what is the bird doing? Is it solitary, gregarious, silent, calling, aggressive, skulking, continually probing or diving, taking short flights, rising and settling again either in flocks or individually, and so on? Any of these characteristics should be entered in your field notebook, as they may be important in turning up the species in a book later on.

HABITAT

This is the place where a bird normally lives – its natural haunts – and is another useful pointer. As you will have read in Chapter Four, birds favour particular types of country or shore, and that is a valuable aid. But we sometimes come across a species quite out of context – an oceanic bird blown far inland by storms; an American species quite out of its usual migratory route; a scarce wader associating with other fairly common visitors. There are, too, plenty of records of flamingos and snow geese, eagles, falcons and owls – all of them obvious escapes from the over-abundant so-called 'wild life' parks that have sprung up of recent years. But you will rarely, if ever, see a curlew in an orchard, or a nightjar in a cornfield – these are not the natural habitat of such birds.

Any 'impossible' or 'improbable' report needs careful investiga-tion and expert opinion before one rushes into print or sends in a record. Mostly birds keep to their natural habitats (which, of course, often change with the seasons) and these often clinch the identification, together with our previous categories of size, shape, posture and behaviour.

LIGHT

The quality of light, or lack of it, together with the time of day and year, can affect the 'appearance' of almost any bird – this is very important. The watcher looking across a sheet of water with a telescope, spots a flock of obvious duck, but what species? The light is poor, the birds look an all-over dull grey or even black. They change direction and they look much lighter; the sun comes out for a brief spell and makes all the difference. They move again – they are up, moving swiftly over the winter sky. What were they? There might have been some 'pattern' on the plumage; their calls, especially those of mallard, wigeon or teal, would have been enough to identify them without anything else. More often than not, they have just 'gone' and unless they circle and come back again, which is very likely, we must put them down as just 'ducks'. There really is no short cut, no easy way, to recognition; one has to watch and watch, make notes, persevere, listen, or move to perhaps some more advantageous viewpoint without disturbing the birds.

It is much more fun with a colleague or two; bird watching is learned more easily and speedily with a companion or a more experienced small group. Stretches of water and miles of shoreland are not the only places where identification is at the mercy of weather, light and season. On the spring moorlands, where the heather is a dark purplish black, even the commonest inhabitant, the meadow pipit, shows up *greenish* against such a background; the colours of small birds beneath the heavy foliage of summer are difficult to determine, and in very many cases one has to rely on calls or songs to correctly identify them.

COLOUR

This has been left to last because it is in most cases the most difficult characteristic, and by now you should be able to identify quite a number of birds without the use of coloured pictures.

Seldom indeed will a bird 'perch' before you in ideal conditions, exactly as you see them in the books. More often than not, a fleeting glimpse, a brief call, is all you get. 'What bird was that?' is an oft-repeated expression among even experienced watchers.

Try, then, to identify all the so-called 'common' birds without reference to any book, merely by size and shape, habitat and behaviour. When you have practised this for some time – and you cannot expect to be able to identify all you see by sight or sound in a couple of months – then you will be more familiar with other species in the same families, and be able to put the unidentified species into its family, whether it be a wader, a gull, or a grebe. That narrows down the field to a group of similar birds.

Your field guide comes in here, and, eliminating the species you know and the species it definitely is *not*, either by size, shape, flight or behaviour, you will be better able to narrow the search down to perhaps one or two species – which is the most likely, taking into consideration time of year, locality, weather and wind, and so on.

Remember, it is not always easy to identify a strange bird; even the experts get confused and disagree at times. So keep to the principles enumerated in this chapter, and don't consult the bird book until you are 'lost'. Fortunately, we have two ways of recognition – sight and sound – and where one is lacking the other may help us. Combining the two methods we shall be able to identify a surprisingly large number of species.

Now look at the twenty-eight birds depicted in silhouette in the following page; don't read any further in this book; study the *shapes* carefully and put down what you think they are. The smaller drawings are not to scale but approximate in size. Award yourself one mark for each correct answer; up to 24 is excellent: up to 18 very good; up to 12, fair. It is only necessary to identify the family, not necessarily the correct species.

Answers on p. 172–3.

NOT TO SCALE

CHAPTER SIX

The birds

Here are brief descriptions and illustrations of the 230 birds in our abbreviated List of British Birds, which includes all the common birds one is likely to encounter, plus some which, although described in the books as 'rare' or 'very local', every bird watcher hopes to see in these islands at least once a lifetime.

If the bird you see is definitely not included here, then one must refer to a field guide, where details of species and distribution will be found. There the descriptions of all those on the British List are amplified and illustrated in colour. The brief details for each species here are the *basic* essentials needed for recognition, and include status, distribution, habitat, features to look for, plus descriptions of voice and calls.

It is not easy to interpret bird sounds into human language. The best one can do is to give an approximation in terms of our tongue, although even then experts may not agree as to the translation. Perhaps the only unmistakable bird in this respect is the cuckoo, whose 'song' everyone knows and recognises, although reports of March cuckoos invariably turn out to be small boys or recordings!

The best course for the beginner is to put his or her interpretation where there is any difficulty; future recognition should then become easier. It takes at least a good season of bird-listening before the beginner can say, without *seeing* the bird, 'that's a willow warbler' or a wren, or a wood lark.

The small drawings are intended to supplement the descriptions by illustrating characteristics of the species, which again can be supplemented by a field guide. These drawings are merely 'keys' or pointers to the family and species. The most important thing to remember is that if your bird does not conform either to description, illustration or voice in this book, then it is maybe another bird of the same family (such as a warbler or wader), and further help is needed. Here is the basic information for the beginner. You will at least be able to put your unknown bird into a category, and this makes it so much easier when wading through the more comprehensive, but necessarily more complicated, field guide.

As far as possible the various 'families' – i.e : warblers, tits, finches, etc. – are drawn in proportionate size so that the species may be instantly recognised. It is of course impossible in any bird book to depict all birds in comparative size, for instance heron and wren would be out of all proportion. 'Size' is from tip of beak to tip of tail.

DIVERS

All ride low in water, as does the cormorant, and only come to land to nest as near water as possible, mainly deep water lochs. All three have a rapid *quack* in flight.

1. *Black-throated diver:* 28 in. Breeds Scotland, winter visitor elsewhere. A black and white bird, back cross-barred, throat black in breeding season, slender straight bill. Weird wailing cries in breeding season.

2. *Great Northern diver:* 30 in. Only winter visitor, occasionally on reservoirs and lakes; black and white pattern. Silent in winter.

3. *Red-throated diver:* 22 in. Breeds Scotland, also winter visitor; red patch on throat in breeding season; slightly upturned bill; longer wing-span than previous two.

GREBES

All grebes are constantly diving, and build floating nests among reeds and rushes. Head patterns should be watched for.

4. *Great Crested grebe:* 20 in. Widely distributed and locally common on large waters. Distinctive ruff and ear-tufts in breeding season, but moulted in winter. Seldom flies. Has delightful courtship displays in late winter, and a series of grunts and 'conversational' notes.

5. *Red-necked grebe:* 17 in. Winter visitor only; can be confused in winter with former, so requires careful observation. Call *kell-kell.*

6. *Slavonian grebe:* 14 in. Breeds Scotland; most colourful grebe in breeding season, sometimes called 'horned'. Trilling call rather like next species in breeding season.

7. *Black-necked grebe:* 12 in. Breeds ponds and reservoirs but very local in England; sometimes colonial breeder where common; rippling 'song'.

8. *Little grebe:* 10 in. Local name is Dabchick. Commonest and smallest grebe, even on small waters which give plenty of cover; a very constant diver; has practically no tail. Rippling call known as 'whickering' often into late summer.

The birds

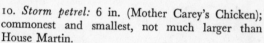

PETRELS

Purely pelagic (i.e. oceanic) birds, only coming to coasts and islands to breed, and only found inland when storm-blown. Nocturnal in breeding season, nesting in burrows and stone walls.

9. *Leach's petrel:* 7½ in. Resident in a few Scottish and Irish islands; flutters low over water. White rump. Sometimes called fork-tailed.

10. *Storm petrel:* 6 in. (Mother Carey's Chicken); commonest and smallest, not much larger than House Martin.

SHEARWATER

Also pelagic birds; only the one species breeds here.

11. *Manx Shearwater:* 14 in. Colonial nester in burrows, often in tens of thousands particularly on Scottish, Welsh and Irish coasts and particularly islands; nocturnal but small numbers seen skimming low over waves (hence name). Weird cries at nesting sites.

FULMARS

12. *Fulmar Petrel:* 18 in. Has colonised east and west coasts of Britain where suitable nest ledges occur; constant gliding flight with few wing-beats, with wings straighter than those of gulls; spends winter at sea; usually a silent bird.

GANNET

13. 30 in. (wing span over 5 ft.). As large as a goose (and called Solan Goose in Scotland); very long beak; white wings, black tipped. Very large colonies: Grassholm (15,000 pairs), St Kilda, Handa, Bass Rock and some fourteen other sites; now spread to Channel Islands. Dives for fish; spends winter at sea; silent except for 'barking' at nest sites.

57

CORMORANTS

14. *Cormorant:* 36 in. Colonial nester all round coasts especially west and Wales; inland, roosts in trees near large sheets of water; one 'inland' breeding site near Towyn, north Wales. Flocks fly in V-formation. Black, white throat, slight crest, swims *very* low in water (hence confusion with divers) and constantly diving for fish; stands with outstretched wings after fishing session; usually silent.

15. *Shag:* 26 in. Much smaller than Cormorant, but also colonial nester; seldom seen inland. Greenish black plumage, no white; silent.

HERON

16. 36 in. Colonial nester in trees, occasionally on ground or on cliffs; often coastal in winter. Grey, white and black with long legs and distinctive black 'crest'. Very slow wing beats (rounded wings); flies with head back behind shoulders, legs outstretched. Call a harsh 'frank'; young very noisy in long nesting period, which begins mid-February. (There are no regular cranes or storks in Britain.)

BITTERN

17. 28 in. Skulking inhabitant of dense reed beds in East Anglia and north Lancashire in breeding season. Mottled and streaked brown and buff plumage closely matching habitat. 'Booming' sound in breeding season rather like fog-horn at sea.

SPOONBILL

18. 34 in. A casual but regular visitor to East Anglia where it formerly bred; white with some 'crest'; long bill with spoonlike end unmistakable. Flies with neck *and* legs outstretched; usually silent.

DUCKS

There are three main types of duck: surface

feeders, usually found in shallows, up-ending and dabbling on surface; bay ducks, diving from the surface and swimming under water; and sea ducks. It is difficult to distinguish *ducks*, as distinct from drakes, or male ducks, unless they are both together, but wing bars and other characteristics are useful. Where large numbers of ducks congregate and are encouraged by visitors – i.e. parks, ornamental waters and collections – hybridisation often takes place and this makes identification more difficult. There are, too, escapees from captivity which have then bred in the wild, such as mandarin or harlequin ducks, and more recently the American 'stiff-tails' which are characterised by upright, pointed tails.

19. *Mallard:* 22 in. The commonest species everywhere and well-known in parks and lakes, augmented in winter by large influxes from the Continent. Glossy green head, white collar, beak yellow, feet orange, with two curly tail feathers unique to this species. Nests near water and sometimes in pollarded trees; calls are *quacks* like domestic species, which are derived from mallard.

20. *Teal:* 14 in. Smallest and fastest duck; large flocks in winter. Unique pattern of head in glossy green and chestnut, yellow-buff under rump very noticeable. Musical *quit-quit* in flight and on water.

21. *Garganey:* 15 in. Local but not rare, chiefly in East Anglia. Prominent white eye-stripe extends to back of neck; male makes clicking sound.

22. *Gadwall:* 19 in. Most soberly-clad of all drakes; thinly distributed and breeds East Anglia. White speculum on wings diagnostic.

23. *Wigeon:* 18 in. Common resident increasing in winter; distinct chestnut head with light orange forehead and crown. Constantly calls *whee-oo, whee-oo* both on water and in flight.

24. *Pintail:* 26 in. Resident but again augmented by winter visitors; unmistakable duck with long neck and pointed white flash on sides, tail long, pointed and elevated (but not to be confused with long-tailed duck, a sea duck). A short whistle.

25. *Shoveler:* 20 in. Widespread resident breeder with glossy green head, chestnut flanks, blue speculum; has broad spatulate bill used to sift water for food and is the only duck with this feature. Some quacking but usually silent.

26. *Scaup:* 18 in. A black maritime duck with some white, breeds locally north Scotland; large flocks around the coasts in winter; a diving duck.

27. *Tufted duck:* 17 in. Possibly the commonest species next to mallard; breeds regularly in suitable spots; black and white with head *crest* rather than a tuft; usually silent bird.

28. *Pochard:* 18 in. Partial migrant, found on large and small lakes, except Wales and south-west England. Uniform dark chestnut head and neck, black breast, white flanks, grey back; a diving or bay duck.

29. *Golden-eye:* 18 in. Winter visitor only, often in large numbers; black and white with distinctive *white* cheek patch and barred black-and-white wings (drake only). Watch for early spring display before they move off (April), throwing their heads back constantly.

30. *Velvet Scoter:* 21 in. Normally a sea duck, winter visitor only; black with white wing patch; a diver; distinct knob on bill.

31. *Common Scoter:* 21 in. Breeds north Scotland but normally winter visitor; only entirely black duck; black bill with bright orange patch and large knob.

32. *Eider-duck:* 24 in. Purely a sea duck, resident and nesting colonially in Scotland, north-west Ireland, Farne Islands, etc. Flocks of thousands in winter, but always a coastal bird. Triangular head in both sexes, striking plumage of drake unmistakable. Courtship call is a rising and falling *oo-OO-oo*.

The next three are sawbills or fish-eating and diving sea ducks.

33. *Red-breasted Merganser:* 23 in. Resident on lochs, spreading south and now nesting north Wales. Drake and duck have distinctive head-dress with double crest – dark green in drake and fawn in duck; latter very like duck Goosander but has less contrasty plumage, and usually the species keep separate. Short quack, but not a noisy bird.

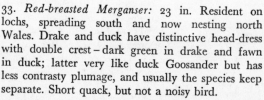

34. *Goosander:* 25 in. Resident in north but not nesting far south. Drake handsome with glossy green head, creamy below, black and white back. Sometimes in small flocks. Quacks like merganser.

35 *Smew:* 16 in. Very distinctive with delicately-patterned black and white, black eye patch; duck black head and darker otherwise. Does not breed here; confined to England in winter as a rule. Normally silent.

36. *Sheld duck:* 25 in. Our largest duck; 'shield' refers to large red knob on drake's bill *only*; striking plumage of green head, uptilted bill; chestnut band on breast; much white on wings and back; sexes almost alike; nests in burrows and dunes around our coasts, occasionally inland.

37. *White-headed duck:* 18 in. This is a 'stiff-tail', with the characteristics upright tail, a species that is becoming a breeding species from wildfowl reserve escapes. The North American ruddy duck belongs to this family, and has the same feature. The white-headed duck has a pale *blue* bill.

38. *Mandarin duck:* 18 in. A most striking drake, quite unmistakable; another species that has become established 'in the wild'. Duck is remarkably unlike drake, but has white eye stripe and surround. Nests in tree holes. A popular bird in wildfowl collections.

GEESE

Recognised by size and flight patterns, often trumpeting or honking in flight, sometimes like a pack of hounds. With exception of Canada goose, wary. Only the latter (and that all over Britain) and Grey lag (in the far north) nest in this country. Sexes are alike.

39. *Grey lag:* 34 in. Our largest goose, and ancestor of farmyard species, resident in Scotland. Only goose with orange bill. Call like domestic species.

40. *White-fronted goose:* 27 in. Two forms (Greenland and Siberian) nesting within the Arctic circle, winter in Britain, the former mainly in Ireland and Scotland, the latter into England and Wales. Both have white front or shield on bill. Black pattern on belly. Flight note is *kow-yow* repeated.

41. *Bean goose:* 32 in. Very dark bird (head and neck almost black at a distance); dark wings in flight; winter visitor only and seldom in large flocks. Low honking calls in flight.

42. *Pink-footed goose:* 28 in. Rather like Bean, but small pink-black bill and pink legs; winter visitor but not Ireland. Call, *wink-wink* or *unk-unk*.

43. *Snow goose:* 28 in. Most visitors here are vagrants, but found increasingly, probably escapees from collections. All-white except for black-tipped wings, pink bill and legs. Harsh call, but as usually solitary is silent.

44. *Brent goose:* 23 in. Our smallest and darkest species (only about size of mallard) and only a winter visitor all over Britain; small patch of white on neck, purely marine and sometimes locally numerous.

45. *Barnacle goose:* 25 in. Local winter visitor only to suitable estuaries and mudflats mainly west Scotland and north west Ireland; very like small Canada goose, but white face and forehead, black breast, grey underparts; rarely found inland. Flock sounds like barking of small dogs.

46. *Canada goose:* 30 in. Widespread introduced species and resident breeder, non migratory, but sometimes moving in large flocks. Common in parks and lakes. Broad white patch from throat to cheek with black head and neck; bill black, brown body, black legs. Flocks call with honk, fly either in V or line formation.

SWANS

47. *Mute swan:* 60 in. Widespread everywhere and 'domesticated' in parks and ornamental waters; resident. Usually holds neck in curve; bill dull red with large black knob. A vegetarian, and has aggressive inclinations in breeding season. Silent save for hissing noises when approached at nesting site or with cygnets. When flying produces a loud singing noise with wings.

48. *Whooper swan:* 60 in. Winter visitor from Arctic tundra to north-east England and Scotland; not Ireland. In hard winters found much farther south on large waters. Long *straight* neck; black bill with large yellow triangle at base. Loud trumpeting call in flight.

49. *Bewick's swan:* 48 in. Also winter visitor, mainly Scotland and Northern Ireland, but found increasingly farther south. Much smaller than whooper and less yellow on bill. Call rather goose-like.

EAGLES

50. *Golden eagle:* 34 in. Largest bird of prey, confined to highlands and remote islands, but recently has bred in Lake District; and usually seen soaring in wild mountainous areas where it breeds. Very broad wings, wing span up to 90 in. with separated primaries; dark brown plumage with golden head and nape; huge yellow hooked bill; legs feathered. Call, a yelping or barking note; harsh screams at nest.

Common Buzzard: 21 in. Resident in wooded and mountainous areas but not eastern England or Ireland. Plumage subject to much variation, habit of soaring continually in good weather, also hovering like kestrel, can identify it. Call, a cat-like mewing on the wing.

52. *Rough-legged buzzard:* 22 in. A much more local species (migratory) frequenting open country as well as marshes; legs feathered to toes; flight and voice rather similar to former.

53. *Sparrow hawk:* male 12 in.; female 15 in. Favours woodland edges and coppices where with swift low flight it pounces on unwary prey, mostly small birds. *Barred* breast, rounded wings, does *not* hover. Call *kek-kek-kek*.

54. *Goshawk:* 20 in. Woodlands, especially conifers, mainly in southern countries; like large Sparrow hawk but *streaked* breast; known to breed sporadically. Often one of a pair is a falconer's escapee; possibly increasing.

55. *Red kite:* 25 in. Now mainly confined to 'hanging' woods of central Wales where there is rigorous protection, but nests elsewhere and straggles widely after breeding season. *Deeply forked* tail and beautiful moth-like plumage, more angular wings than buzzard, but similar call.

56. *Marsh harrier:* 24 in. Usually haunts reed beds and dense marshes in East Anglia, but sometimes does not nest at all; very uncertain. Flies low; no white rump; a much heavier bird than the following two, and slow wing beats. Said to have whistling call in breeding season.

57. *Hen harrier:* 20 in. Prefers open moorland; regular in north Scotland and beyond; sparingly elsewhere. Male pale grey with black wing tips and conspicuous white trump; female streaked brown, with white rump. Call *kek-kek-kek*. (This is a common note of many birds of prey.)

58. *Montagu's harrier:* 18 in. Confined mostly to heaths and downs in England, but still a scarce breeding bird, mainly in the south. Male smaller and slimmer than Marsh harrier; off-white rump; female much like female hen harrier but can be confused with latter. Call *kek-kek-kek*, higher tone than other harriers'.

59. *Osprey:* 23 in. Fish hawk, always nesting in tall trees above water on large lochs; increasingly breeding in Scotland. Distinct facial pattern and much white underneath; easily recognised in flight. Has shrill mewing cry.

60. *Hobby:* 12 in. Open woodlands or isolated clumps, mainly in southern England; likes woodland rides for hunting; looks very like large swift in flight, with long pointed wings; distinctive facial pattern; heavily marked breast. Often uses crow's old nest. Call *keek-eek-eek*.

61. *Peregrine:* 20 in. Largest, swiftest and most handsome of all our falcons; now much reduced in numbers due to pesticides and persecution. Has nested all over Britain, mainly on sea cliffs but also inland where there is a good wide look-out from the eyrie. Sharply pointed wings; strong facial with 'moustachial' stripes; barred and spotted underparts. Flies with rapid wing beats before 'stooping' on prey, usually pigeons but also ducks. Call: *hek-hek-hek*; especially noisy when disturbed at nest site.

The birds

62. *Merlin:* 11 in. Smallest falcon, confined to open moorlands and hillsides; nests on ground or in old tree nests. Rapid flier low over heather; male bluish back, female brown, both with pointed wings. Call: *kik-ik-ik-ik.*

63. *Kestrel:* 13 in. Commonest bird of prey anywhere in all types of country, on farmlands and edges of woods. Only hawk that constantly hovers, hence 'windhover'. Pointed wings, unlike Sparrow hawk; strongly streaked breast. Male blue head, reddish back, black band on tail; female brown mottled and streaked. Call: *kwee-kwee-kwee.*

GROUSE

64. *Red Grouse:* 14 in. Resident on heather moors and spreading to non-heather areas; scarce in south and south-east but regular in Wales, north England and Ireland. Plump dark rufous bird with red wattle; typically noisy at start of breeding season; found only in Britain; several guttural calls and well-known *go-back, go-back-go-back-back.*

65. *Ptarmigan:* 14 in. The grouse of the Highland mountain tops, strikingly marked with white and blackish-brown; all white in winter. Has odd croaking noises.

66. *Black Grouse:* 22 in. Bird of scrub and woodland fringes, especially young conifers, at foot of which it nests. Very distinctive pattern, largely black and white in flight, with lyre-shaped tail. Increasing in forestry plantations, including England and Wales. 'Leks' take place in spring where large numbers assemble for display in early morning. A polygamous bird. Calls: mostly bubbling and cooing at leks, but sometimes in daytime.

67. *Capercaillie:* 35 in. Largest and heaviest of the 'game' family, favouring coniferous woods, especially those of Rothiemurchus. Bursts out of cover with rocket-like suddenness. Has unique 'crows', and scraping noises with widespread tail.

67

PARTRIDGES

68. *Red-legged partridge:* 14 in. Also called French partridge. Farmlands and heaths, mainly southern part of England and Wales; slightly plumper than common partridge, with striking head and breast pattern. Reluctant to fly, hence not popular with keepers. Call like labouring steam engine – *chu-chuck-chi-chuck-chi-chuck.*

69. *Common Partridge:* 12 in. Mainly farm land and open countryside; often in coveys; flies like grouse with down-curved wings. Churring calls – *cair-witt, cair-witt,* especially before going to roost.

70 *Quail:* 7 in. Smallest gamebird. Very local summer visitor to all parts and possibly increasing; farmlands especially barley fields, but rarely if ever seen. Calls night and day; most books say *wet-my-lips* but to author it is *kik-wikwikwik, wik wikwik.*

71. *Common Pheasant:* 32 in. Deciduous woods and rides, increasingly hand-reared; unmistakable with extraordinarily long tail; one variety has white ring round neck. Call, a harsh *kok-kok* and noisy in flight.

RAILS

72. *Water Rail:* 10 in. Reed beds, boggy banks of pools and streams, skulking but often noisy; long reddish bill, barred flanks. Call *jik-jik-jik* with sundry pig-like squeals from cover.

73. *Corncrake:* 10 in. Also called Land-rail. A skulker in cornfield and hayfield *seldom seen* and sparingly recorded; not south and south-east England. Possibly increasing slightly; unmistakable call *crekcrek – crekcrek,* often all night until mid-July. Summer visitor only.

68

74. *Moorhen:* 13 in. More properly *mere*hen or waterhen; commonest water-bird found everywhere even on smallest pond. Bobs head in swimming, and flicks tail when walking, showing white underparts. Red shield above beak. Has numerous calls and hiccoughs.

75. *Coot:* 16 in. Very common but on larger waters than moorhen, often in big winter flocks. No white on plumage but has white shield above beak. Has explosive and metallic calls.

OYSTERCATCHER
76. 16 in. A misnomer as species eats cockles and mussels; also called seapie. Mainly coastal but now breeding inland on shingle in Scottish rivers. Not found Ireland or southern England. Conspicuous black-and-white bird with long orange bill and long pink legs and feet. Very large flocks in winter on estuaries, etc. Noisy bird at all times with musical notes, and call of *kleep – kleep.*

LAPWING
77. 13 in. Also called peewit or green plover. Open country, marshes, farmland. Only wader with *rounded* wings in flight and conspicuous black and white plumage; long narrow crest. Large flocks in winter often including golden plover, *q.v.* Usual call *pee-ee-wit,* often restless at night when roosting. Wild spring flight with 'wuff-wuff' of wings and frenzied *will-o-weeit, willock-o-weeit, peeo-weet.*

PLOVERS
78. *Ringed Plover:* 7 in. Mainly coastal, nesting on sand or shingle, flocking on estuaries in winter. Runs rapidly across sand as though on wheels. Distinct white wing bar in flight. Call, *pee-ip, pee-ip.*

79. *Little Ringed Plover:* 6 in. Increasing inland, especially old gravel pits and reservoir edges, shingle beds in rivers. *No* white wing bar in flight.

80. *Grey Plover:* 12 in. Winter visitor only in small groups locally on mudflats and estuaries, therefore in winter plumage. Call, *pee-u-wee*.

81. *Golden Plover:* 10 in. High moorlands, Scotland, Ireland, Pennines and scattered north Wales; large flocks in winter and much farther south than Pennines; often associated with lapwings but distinctly smaller size, black-and-gold mottled plumage, pointed wings and V-formation in flight. Difficult to see on ground. Call *tloo-ee* and attractive *kloo-klee, kloo-klee* in breeding season.

82. *Dotterel:* 9 in. Only on tundra on high mountains above 3,000 ft.; unmistakable plumage pattern and only bird of its size in habitat. Remarkably tame; male only incubates. Found on hilltops farther south on migration.

TURNSTONE

83. 9 in. Winter visitor to all coasts, non-breeders often staying over summer. Distinctive 'tortoise-shell' plumage and individual method of turning over seaweed and stones for food. Metallic alarm note when flying.

SNIPE

84. *Common snipe:* 10 in. Boggy uplands, wet meadows and marshes everywhere in breeding season, flocking in winter. Zig-zag flight with *scaape-scaape* note. Male bleats or drums by towering up and dropping with goat-like sound produced by vibration of outer tail feathers. Also calls *chipper-chipper* from ground or post near nest.

70

The birds

The *jack snipe,* smaller, is a winter visitor, more or less solitary. Flight not so zig-zag, no call, and soon returns to same spot, usually at streamside. (No figure.)

WOODCOCK

85. 13 in. Deciduous woods with good ground cover of leaves and bracken; not far from boggy feeding grounds, which it visits usually at dusk. Has 'roding' flight along defined paths, with bill pointed downwards, uttering a hoarse croak. Large flocks arrive in autumn.

CURLEWS

86. *Curlew:* 23 in. Hilltops and open moorlands, but spreading to lower land (often arable) in breeding season. Widespread in Britain, more numerous in north; in winter large flocks on estuaries and mudflats all round coast. Easily distinguished by long curved bill (9 in.) – but see Whimbrel following – and constant 'coorlee' cries at all seasons. Delightful bubbling song in spring. Often heard on migration at night.

87. *Whimbrel:* 17 in. More a northern breeder (far north of Scotland, Orkney and Shetland). Smaller than last bird but similar in shape and bill; distinct eye stripes identify. Often associated with curlew on estuaries and then easily compared. Called 'seven-whistler' from its typical note *hew-hew-hew* repeated 6 or 7 times, often at night.

GODWITS

88. *Black-tailed godwit:* 18 in. Bird of mudflats, coastal marshes and estuaries; long straight bill, white wing bars (in flight), white rump and broad black band on tail. Now breeding under protection Ouse and Welney Washes. Call, *wikka-wikka.*

89. *Bar-tailed godwit:* 15 in. Arctic breeder; closely packed flocks here in winter; white rump but barred tail pattern and no white wing bars. Call: *wick-wick.*

SANDPIPERS

90. *Green sandpiper:* 9 in. Winter visitor only and local on marshes, sewage farms and shoreland, often singly or small parties. Looks black and white in flight, with white rump; often flies high. Call, *klu-wee.*

91. *Wood sandpiper:* 8 in. Winter visitor in marshy land and sewage farms, etc. Very mottled plumage, yellow legs. Triple call, *giff-giff-giff.*

92. *Common sandpiper:* 8 in. Summer visitor and breeder, commonest of all sandpipers, except southeast England and East Anglia. Mountain streams and riversides, also wetlands in lower country. 'Rocks' body to and fro while walking and shows much white underneath; white bar on wings in flight. Shrill *dee-dee-dee,* and brief rippling song in territory.

93. *Redshank:* 10 in. Fairly common in lowland meadows and marshes, also edges of moorland. White wing bars and rump conspicuous in flight; red legs; Large winter flocks. Noisy bird in breeding season (hence name 'warden of the marshes') getting up before any other bird and yelping *tew-hee-hee.* Loud alarm *teuk-teuk-teuk.*

94. *Spotted Redshank:* 12 in. Non-breeding winter visitor; very dark, white-spotted plumage, red legs. Singly or in small numbers. Call: *tewit, tewit.*

95. *Greenshank:* 13 in. Open moorland and near pinewoods in north Scotland, but coming farther south in winter. Greenish legs, white rump, barred tail in flight; slightly upturned bill. Loud *chew-chew-chew* in nesting area.

KNOTS, STINTS

96. *Knot:* 10 in. Winter visitor only to estuaries and mudflats, often closely packed in tens of thousands. Feeds along shoreline moving slowly, when grey mottled plumage and whitish underparts can be seen. Short bill. Hoarse *kut-kut* call.

97. *Purple sandpiper:* 8 in. Winter visitor to coasts, also sewage farms and reservoirs, but not in large flocks. Very dark bird with deeply mottled grey plumage. Often seen with turnstones on rocky shores. Call, *wit-wit.*

Little

Temminck's

98. *Little stint:* 6 in. Arctic breeder often found in mixed wader flocks on mudflats and estuaries. Very tiny and difficult to pick out, but smaller than dunlin and more brown on lighter plumage; thin white wing bar in flight and white outer-tail feathers. Call, *twicky-twick.*

98a. *Temminck's stint:* 6 in. Also Arctic breeder found in similar places to former, but difficult to distinguish; much greyer all over than little stint, and voice different: a short trill rather than triple call.

99. *Dunlin:* 7 in. Breeds on moors and uplands especially Pennines and farther north, sparingly in Wales but not below Severn to Wash line. Commonest small wader, recognised in breeding season by distinct black belly and brown-grey plumage; in winter loses black patch but sometimes traces are left; in winter found on sewage farms and around small pools. Usually fairly approachable if care is taken. Winter note *trerr;* trilling song in breeding area, usually in flight.

100. *Curlew sandpiper:* 7 in. Winter visitor on shores, mudflats and sewage farms, chiefly east coast but often inland. Slightly down-curved bill, pinkish tinged plumage in winter, white rump. Has lark-like chirrup.

101. *Sanderling:* 8 in. Winter visitor to shores and mudflats; whitest of all small waders, and feeds fast close to edge to tideline, often in large flocks. Call in flight, *plick-plick.*

RUFF (female Reeve)

102. 12 in. Summer visitor, formerly bred East Anglia in marshes and coastal meadows and washes, and now returned under protection. Totally different in breeding and winter plumage; latter mottled and scaly-looking upper parts, but variable. Males assume distinctive 'ruffs' in breeding season, with no two alike, plumage ranging from almost black to almost white, used in striking displays. Rather silent bird.

AVOCET

103. 17 in. to 18 in. Now returned to breed East Anglia in shallow lagoons after absence of 100 years. Unmistakable bird with strong black and white contrasted plumage, long legs and unique upturned bill used to sift water in feeding; also distinctive in flight. Winters on south coast, particularly Cornwall. Call, *klu-it.*

PHALAROPES

The next two birds are nearly always on water, and feed with unusual habit of turning round and round, stirring up water creatures for food.

104. *Grey phalarope:* 8 in. Winter visitor from Iceland, singly or small flocks; a grey bird with white breast and belly, needle-thin bill; Call, *whit-whit,* sometimes noisy in flocks.

105. *Red-necked phalarope:* 7 in. Breeds sparingly in small groups in marshes, lakes and islands, north Scotland and Ireland; bright chestnut band on neck; dark head, white chin in breeding season. Call, *plip-plip.*

74

STONE CURLEW

106. 16 in. Summer visitor to East Anglia, very local elsewhere, dry heaths, sandy wastes, chalk downs, etc. Strongly streaked plumage, large yellow eyes, very shy and active nocturnally; distinct double white bars on wings, and slow flight. Calls *coor-lee* at dusk, otherwise silent.

SKUAS

These are purely marine pirates, preying on terns and smaller gulls, forcing them to drop their fish. Distinct flight pattern, angular wings with white fleshes, and elongated central tail feathers. Immature birds very difficult; usually silent but will attack intruders at nests.

107. *Arctic skua:* 18 in. Usually seen on autumn migration and commonest following flocks of terns and gulls down our coasts. Elongated but straight central tail feathers distinguish it from other species; very dark plumage with white splashes in flight, but variable; usually seen off-shore.

108. *Great skua:* 23 in. Largest species, breeds Orkney and Shetland, but travels to Spain and Mediterranean outside breeding season; also breeds Antarctica. Short tail, hooked black bill, and wings rounded and broad unlike other skuas. Usually solitary.

109. *Long-tailed skua:* 21 in. Much longer tail projections than other species; less white on wings than last two and much whiter underneath.

GULLS

There are seven common British species, easy to recognise in adult stage, but immature birds are very difficult unless importuning parents for food, as they are mottled brown birds, often with black beak and legs quite unlike adults. Nominally sea birds breeding on or near coasts they are (especially black-headed, herring and so-called common gull) increasingly inland breeders, and now found on rubbish tips and following farm tractors everywhere. Often seen soaring very high, but light under-plumage and numbers usually distinguish them.

110. *Greater Black-backed gull:* 28 in. to 30 in. Largest of all, with really *black* back and massive yellow bill. Often preys on bird colonies, but so do lesser black-backed and herring gulls; pink legs. Usual voice a barking *owk-owk-owk*. Breeds all round coast, especially in high situations and on rocky islands.

111. *Lesser Black-backed gull:* 21 in. Has *dark grey* back, yellow bill and legs; breeds colonially in large numbers (Walney Island, the largest colony in Europe). Typical gull cries but not so deep as former species.

112. *Herring gull:* 22 in. *Pale grey* back; commonest seaside gull; yellow beak but flesh-coloured legs. Has 'laughing' calls and *kyow* note.

113. *Common gull:* 16 in. Actually least common species; breeds in large colonies inland in Northern Ireland, Scotland and on moors; only one colony England (Dungeness). Pale grey upper parts, black band on tail; greenish bill and legs. Higher voice than herring gull.

Glaucous gull: 27 in. A non-breeding winter visitor included here because increasingly reported in winter gull flocks; no black at all; grey back and wings; pink legs, yellow bill. Calls as herring gull. (Iceland gull is similar but smaller and even scarcer.) (No figure.)

114. *Black-headed gull:* 15 in. Possibly commonest species, increasingly nesting inland sometimes in large colonies on moorlands. Chocolate-coloured hood in breeding season, coral red bill and legs, but only a black spot behind the eye in winter, otherwise white with grey back. Many calls, sounding querulous and aggressive, especially at nests.

The birds

KITTIWAKE

115. 16 in. Purely a *sea* gull, migratory, nesting on steep cliffs and rocky coasts all round Britain except in south-east and East Anglia. Yellow bill, black legs. Immature birds have black and white pattern on head and neck. Unmistakable cries, *kittiwake-kittiwake.*

TERNS

Graceful birds easily distinguished as such; often called sea swallows by reason of typical long pointed wings and tail; nearly always over water, plunging in for small fish and sand eels; all have very short legs, hover, and much alike in flight, but study calls.

116. *Black tern:* 10 in. Mainly spring and autumn passage migrant, usually over inland waters and meres, but now breeding sparingly Ouse Washes. Blackish breeding plumage; white under tail; black bill. Builds floating nest. Call, *kit-kit,* but not a noisy species.

117. *Common tern:* 14 in. Summer visitor almost purely coastal England and Wales but inland Scotland and Ireland. Grey back and wings; orange red bill with black tip; black crest; nests colonially. A noisy species, with grating calls. *pee-er* or *kee-urr* or *kit-kit-kit.*

118. *Arctic tern:* 15 in. Summer visitor with grey back and wings, black head, but beak wholly blood red. Purely coastal British Isles, in large colonies, i.e.: Farne Islands. Calls like common species but possibly more rasping and harsh.

119. *Roseate tern:* 15 in. Rarest of species breeding here (but see next species); sometimes nests within other tern colonies. Rosy tinge on breast difficult to see; bill black with red base. Call. *kraark,* kraark, also chatter *kekekek.*

120. *Little tern:* 9 in. Smallest species. Breeds in scattered colonies on beaches all round our coasts but seriously declining due to human pressure on nesting sites. Has white forehead, black eye stripe through eye, yellow bill and legs. Very 'chattery' tern, with rapid harsh notes.

121. *Sandwich tern:* 16 in. Largest species. Breeds in crowded colonies all round coasts except Wales, southern England and south-west Ireland. Large black bill with yellow tip; black legs; heavy elongated crest larger than other terns. Call, rasping *kirrick, kirrik.*

AUKS

The next five birds only come ashore during the breeding season, except when gale-driven inland by storms, when they usually perish. They fly low over water, dive for fish, and the first four stand over their single egg like penguins. Puffins breed in burrows. All are coastal breeders.

122. *Razorbill:* 16 in. Black back, white underparts; heavy-looking bill with vertical white streaks, white horizontal line on wings. Nearest relative of extinct great auk. Little sound heard as a rule.

Little auk: 8 in. Only auk which does not breed here, but on Arctic cliffs in vast numbers; only found in Britain after storms, usually irregularly in English Channel. (No figure.)

123. *Guillemot:* 17 in. Similar haunts to Razorbill, but often steeper, narrower cliffs. Long pointed bill; narrow white band on wings. Also a 'bridled' variety with white streak behind eye. Call, *arrr-arrr.*

124. *Black guillemot:* 13 in. Bird of north and western British shores only; all black except large white *patch* on wing; distinctive red gape; winter flocks at sea very white and mottled, but white wing patch remains.

78

125. *Puffin:* 12 in. Most distinctive of auks; stumpy shape, black and white plumage, legs orange. Bill has horny layer or red, yellow and blue in breeding season, but sheds this in winter. Breeds very large colonies all round coasts but not east and south-east England. Numbers diminishing. Call, guttural *ow-ow* and *arr*.

DOVES
There are five doves or pigeons, all resident except turtle dove. All have distinctive calls.

126. *Stock dove:* 13 in. Common in wooded areas much as wood pigeon, but is a much smaller bird with *no white* patches. Nests in tree holes usually. Call, *coo-ook, coo-ook*.

127. *Rock dove:* 13 in. Rarest species and now only found north Scotland and Ireland; interbreed with feral (domestics gone wild) pigeons therefore true race is being lost. Dark blue with heavy black bands on wings, much like many homing pigeons, white rump. Ancestor of all domestic types. Call, *oo-roo-coo*, like domestic birds.

128. *Wood pigeon:* 16 in. Quice or ring dove. Largest and commonest of all, found everywhere; nests trees, bushes and buildings, vastly reinforced in winter by Continental flocks. White patches on neck and wings; often makes noisy flapping sounds; soars and drops with wings closed. Call, *coocoo-coo-coo-coo* usually ending with *ook*; also has crooning note.

129. *Collared dove:* 11 in. Newcomer to Britain from East; now resident and breeding everywhere; has reached west coast of Ireland. Cinammon plumage, half-black 'ring' at back of neck, bordered white. Tail shows much white. Call, *coo-COO-cook, coo-COO-cook*, and has harsh 'alighting' call.

130. *Turtle dove:* 11 in. Only true migrant, a summer visitor, arriving mid-May. Nests in coppices and light deciduous woods. Black streaks at *side* of neck, much white on tail. Call, purring *roo-cooo-roo-cooo* or *turr-turrturr,* hence name.

CUCKOO

131. 13 in. Summer visitor to all parts; grey (but also a reddish phase), long, pointed wings, barred breast; long well-marked tail. Adults leave July-September, juveniles much later, up to October. Call, well-known, but stutter occurs in June, *cuck-cuck-oo,* sometimes only *cuck.* Female has bubbling note.

OWLS

Six species can be claimed as reasonable to encounter, but there are thirteen on the European list, some of which are mere stragglers here.

132. *Barn owl:* 14 in. Also White or Screech owl. Usually near farms, where it formerly nested in barns (some buildings even had 'owl' holes for them). Hunts at dusk, looking very white, with distinct facial mask, hawking low and quartering field for mice and voles. Has skriek, hisses at nest, and an almost human snore.

133. *Snowy owl:* 24 in. Included because it has now bred for some time in the Orkneys; mainly an Arctic bird occurring nevertheless as a vagrant elsewhere.

134. *Little owl:* 9 in. Smallest species, introduced and now spreading towards Scotland, but not Ireland. Often seen on telephone poles in broad day. Fierce expression, and has 'bobbing' action. Call, shrill *kee-yoo.*

Eider-duck sitting on her nest in the Farne Islands (owned by the National Trust). One can approach such sitting birds closely, but they should never be disturbed or touched

Newly-fledged Swallows in a house porch. Taken with flash-bulb at 2 ft.

Blue Tit at home-made nest box. Taken by remote control and flash-bulb

Gannets on Grassholm, an R.S.P.B. reserve. Neither hide nor telephoto lens is needed for such pictures

Nest of the Whiskered Tern, floating on lily leaves. Taken in central France from a punt

Nest of Little Ringed Plover on shingle on the river Loire, France. Taken by paddling through shallow water

Nest of Mistle Thrush in garden. This sort of picture can be taken with almost any type of camera

Another nest picture (that of the Common Tern) taken with a simple camera on a Norfolk bird reserve

Dead Gannet picked up in a mass of Bladder Campion on the Farne Islands.
The nearest colony is Bass Rock. Taken with Silette camera

Patience and slow movements are necessary for such garden pictures. Robin
feeding from hand

Song Thrush 'lured' to snail on lawn. The camera was placed on two bricks, pre-focused and shutter released by remote control

A unique flash photograph which took the author a whole winter to secure. Coal Tit, Blue Tit and Great Tit together on a peanut feeder

Black-headed Gulls in flight at nesting site in Wales. Such pictures require high-speed exposures (250th sec. minimum) and accurate metering. Taken with standard 50mm lens

Canada Goose's nest on island, taken from punt. Pictures like this are easy with almost any apparatus provided exposure and distances are accurately calculated

Great-crested Grebe's nest camouflaged
by parent before leaving

Nest uncovered to show chalky eggs.
Cover was carefully replaced before
leaving since minimum disturbance is
necessary. Both taken from a punt

135. *Tawny owl:* 15 in. Or Brown owl. Woods, parkland, hollow trees, but sometimes nests on ground. Handsome mottled and streaked brown plumage. Seen in daytime close to trunk of tree, when often mobbed by noisy small birds. Only owl that really *hoots, hoo-hoohooho-hoo-oo,* ending in a quavering note. Female and young, *keewick, keewick.* Noisy during October and November when young driven from home ground. Tawny owls will attack humans getting too near their nesting sites.

136. *Long-eared owl:* 14 in. Only species with long 'ear' tufts; favours coniferous woods where breeds in old crows' nests. Very local. Call, low *oo-oo-oo;* young noisy in nest.

137. *Short-eared owl:* 15 in. Owl of open moorland, hunting by day as well as dusk; ear tufts normally not conspicuous. Has distinctive facial mask; longish barred wings. Scotland, north England and Eat Anglia, local elsewhere. Usually silent but a dog-like bark is recorded.

NIGHTJAR

138. 10 in. Summer visitor, active only after dusk; silent and roosting by day, when perches parallel with branch; favours birch-and-bracken or dune habitats, borders of moorland; nest on ground. Like gigantic silent moth in flight; flaps wings together over back. Churrs incessantly and loudly. sometimes running-down like clockwork toy. Calls *coo-ick* in flight.

SWIFT

139. 7 in. Related to above and not to swallow family; summer visitor arriving May and departing mid-August. Plentiful in old towns and villages, also ruins. Sleeps and mates on the wing, and only comes to nesting site (dark holes) to make nest and incubate and feed young; cannot perch. Long scythe-like wings (it cannot take off from the ground), sooty-black plumage. Have high-pitched *swee-ree, swee-ree* as they chase each other round buildings and towers.

KINGFISHER

140. 7 in. Resident, and our most brilliant and unmistakable bird with metallic blue back, brick-red underparts, white flashes on throat and neck; often seen just disappearing up or down stream as a streak of blue. Favours slow rivers and streams with suitable bank for nesting hole, which it usually excavates itself. Reports of increases in some areas after bad contamination disasters. Has whistling note in flight – *zeek*; said to have infrequent song.

HOOPOE

141. 11 in. Included because regularly reported every spring especially East Anglia, and has bred. Unmistakable crest (which can be raised or depressed); long curved beak; strongly barred black and white wings and tail. 'Butterfly' flight. Distinctive call, *oop-poo-poo.*

WOODPECKERS

142. *Green woodpecker:* 13 in. Also Yaffle and Uckle-bird. Largest British species, in mature woods and parks, sometimes old orchards; absent Scotland and Ireland. Bright green back, red crown, black eye patch, yellow rump. Strong bounding flight. In sunlight easily mistaken for Golden Oriole, *q.v.* Fond of probing ant nests in woodland. Loud laughing cry, *yah-yah-yah-yah.*

143. *Pied woodpecker:* 9 in. Or Great Spotted woodpecker. Conspicuous black and white bird with red patch on nape (male only), in same haunts as above but absent Ireland. Mechanical 'song' by rapidly vibrating bill on bare tree branch, usually high up, spring only. Call, *chek . . . chek.* Flight as green species.

144. *Barred woodpecker:* 6 in. Or Lesser Spotted woodpecker. Smallest and scarcest of family, but can be overlooked owing to quiet unobtrusive habits. Haunts much like former two. Closely barred back, dull red crown; scarcely larger than a sparrow. Rare north England and not Ireland. Drums less strongly than last named, and has weak call, *kee-kee-kee.*

The birds

WRYNECK

145. 7 in. Or Cuckoo's Mate. Summer visitor, now confined to woodlands in extreme south-east England, where decreasing. Unobtrusive bird with mottled and vermiculated brown plumage; climbs like woodpecker, and twists head round. Call, a *very loud* ringing *kew-kew-kew* unlikely to be overlooked in spring.

LARKS

146. *Wood lark:* 6 in. Parklands and hillsides with mature trees and now confined to southern half of England and Wales, where very local since 1963 winter. Stumpier than skylark, perches in trees, from which it rises in spiral, coming back to tree again, often singing after dark. Beautiful flute-like notes unlike skylark, more pauses and typical *loo-loo-loo* phrase repeatedly used.

147. *Skylark:* 7 in. Open country, fields, crops, moors and downs everywhere. Look for white tail margins, and typical lark note in winter flocks. Erect crest, sings in the air for minutes on end, but also from post or on ground. Longest continuous song of any British bird. Call, *chirr-up.*

148. *Shore lark:* 7 in. Winter visitor only, mainly east coast; distinct facial pattern and yellowish patches on chin and cheeks. Male crest less obvious in winter. Call, tsee-tsee but song said to be inferior to last two.

SWALLOWS

149. *Swallow:* 8 in. Summer visitor widespread over Britain; note chestnut-red forehead and throat and metallic blue back; long tail streamers (not so obvious in juveniles). Nests *inside* buildings on beams and ledges, sometimes old chimneys; large reed roosts in autumn before departure. Song a pleasing warbling mixture with rapid twittering.

83

150. *House martin:* 5 in. Also widespread summer visitor; black above with white rump; white breast, fish-tail; nests *outside* buildings under eaves and bridge arches, locally on cliffs as in prehistoric times; sometimes large colonies. Has weak song and chirruping less varied than swallow.

151. *Sand martin:* 4¾ in. Widespread summer visitor to river banks, sand pits, cliffs, nesting in deep bored tunnels colonially. Smallest of family, mouse-brown upper parts with brown band across chest. Short chirruping at nest sites.

GOLDEN ORIOLE
152. 9½. Occasional but regular summer visitor to east coast and elsewhere: wooded areas, parks, large gardens and orchards. Brilliant yellow plumage with black wings and tail; not red on head like green woodpecker. Keeps well hidden in tree tops as a rule, but flies in long undulations like woodpecker. Song a fluty *weela-weeoo*, and harsh churring call.

CROWS
153. *Raven:* 24 in. Resident in mountains and remote valleys, cliffs and wooded hills all over Britain except east and south-east England. Largest crow, with all-black plumage, heavy pick-axe bill, broad wings with spread primaries in flight. Important feature in flight – tail is *wedge*-shaped. Often tumbles and somersaults in air, closing wings and diving. Nesting begins February. Calls, hoarse *prruk-prruk*, with pig-like grunts and clucking noises, unlike other crows.

154. *Carrion crow:* 18 in. Common all over Britain but not Ireland. Usually solitary; smaller than raven and with *square* tail in flight. Nests in trees and on cliffs often far from human habitation. Typical note, *kraa-kraa-kraa*.

155. *Hooded crow:* 18 in. Really a sub-species of above and found more commonly in north Scotland and Ireland. Grey and black plumage distinguish. Habits and calls as Carrion crow.

156. *Rook:* 18 in. Gregarious at all times all over Britain; nests in rookeries, and roosts in large numbers in winter, often with jackdaws, which are also associated with in the fields. Has 'plus fours' unlike the other crows, and a whitish, pointed beak bare at the base through probing, but young have beaks like carrions. Noisy birds in rookeries and flocks, with loud *caw-caw-caw*.

157. *Jackdaw:* 13 in. Smallest black bird of family, frequenting old buildings, cliffs, farms, ruins, all over country. Greyish patch on nape; bright blue eye; often associated with rooks and starlings feeding in fields. Call, *jack, jackajack*, and *keeah*.

158. *Magpie:* 18 in. (including tail of 9 in.). Farms, open country, woodlands, parks, etc. Glossy plumage – long greenish tail and bluish wings and distinct white patch on belly. Often seen in small parties. Builds its own domed nest in thorn or other tree. Has loud chattering or rattling alarm often repeated when humans about. A persistent egg thief.

159. *Jay:* 14 in. The handsomest bird of coniferous and deciduous woods and coppices. Pinkish plumage with black tail, white chin and white patch on wings; mottled head and blue-black barred feathers in wings, but conspicuous white rump is usually sufficient identification when flying away. Silent while nesting, but first bird to be heard out of season, when a harsh *shraa-ak* warns other birds (and gamekeepers) of man's presence. Another persistent egg thief.

CHOUGH

160. 15 in. Very local indeed and probably decreasing on coasts, rocky cliffs, old ruins and islands, now confined to west and north Wales, Calf of Man, west Scotland and western Ireland; once common now rare in Cornwall. Long curved red bill, red legs and very widespread primaries in flight, plus call *kee-ah, kee-ah* identify it.

TITMICE

161. *Great tit:* 6 in. Widespread everywhere; sulphur underparts with black band down centre; blue-black head and neck; largest species. Many calls, often beginning mid-winter, strong and loud bell-like, *teacher-teacher, teeteeacher* and many others. Most versatile vocabulary of all the tits.

162. *Blue tit:* 4½ in. Or Tomtit. Commonest everywhere even in town gardens and readily accepts nesting boxes. *Blue* cap identifies; black eyestripe and bib; yellow underparts. Call, high pitched *tsee-tsee.* Song, *tsee-tsee-tisit-tisit.*

163. *Coal tit:* 4¼ in. More of a woodland bird, especially conifers; black head with white cheek and nape of neck; greyer than Blue tit; nests in holes close to ground, often under tree roots or in a wall crevice; comes to gardens in winter. Song, *weechoo, weechoo,* or *ifhee, ifhee.* Call, thin *tsee, tsee.*

164. *Crested tit:* 4¼ in. Confined to coniferous (Scots pine) woods in Rothiemurchus Forest, where resident. Prominent speckled upright crest and black and white facial pattern; brown back, wings and tail. Has purring trill. Call is as Coal tit.

86

165. *Marsh tit:* 4½ in. Resident England and Wales only, woods, edges of parklands, thickets. By no means a marsh bird. *Shining* black head; sooty brown back, wings with no light patch. Difficult to tell from next species in poor light unless very close. Calls, *pitychoo-pitychoo* and *chay-chay-chay.* Little 'song'.

166. *Willow tit:* 4½ in. Same distribution as above but perhaps denser thickets and damper places, where often heard but unseen. Has *dull* black head and faint light patch on wings. Call of *chay-chay-chay* sounds really nasal. Excavates own nest in rotten stump.

167. *Long-tailed tit:* 5½ in. including tail. Quite unmistakable; prefers hedgerows, gorse bushes, etc., where plenty of rough cover; purely insectivorous and builds own nest of moss, lichen and feathers in thorn or bramble bush. Nest is rounded, with entrance hole near top. Family parties often keep together and often associated with goldcrests and other tits in winter. Has thin reedy *tzee-tzee* typical of most tits. Harsh call *tupp-tupp.*

168. *Bearded tit:* 6½ in. Also Bearded Reedling or Reed Pheasant. Confined to broads, etc., where there is *Phragmites* Reed in which it feeds and nests. Population explosions sometimes take them to widespread localities in winter, but always in similar habitat. Unmistakable birds with handsome black moustaches; very long tail. Has no song. Call, a ringing *ping-ping-ping.*

NUTHATCH

169. 5½ in. Mature oak and beech woods, parks, large gardens. Handsome bird with slate-blue back, pale orange belly, white throat and black eyestripe. Climbs up or down tree trunks; makes nesting hole to fit either by chipping out or plastering up with mud. All songs or calls are sheer whistles often like man calling a dog, and cheerful sounding notes. Call, *twit-twit-twit.* There are several variations. Not Scotland or Ireland.

TREE CREEPER

170. 5 in. Any type of mature woodland, parks, large gardens, where it is an unobtrusive brown-speckled bird looking like a piece of bark climbing up a tree. Usually goes so far up a trunk and then drops down to the base of a nearby tree, but often seen high up, and difficult to spot. Song, a thin high-pitched *see-see-sissy-see* (like goldcrest). Feeble call, *tsee-tsee.*

WREN

171. 4 in. Widely distributed bird with subspecies in Shetlands, St Kilda and elsewhere. Found in all types of country from town gardens to wild hillsides and rocky valleys. Brown with cocked short tail; always searching for food, mainly spiders and insects. Very loud song of quick, clear notes ending in a rattle. Call, usually a loud *tit-tit-tit.*

DIPPER

172. 7 in. Found in most valleys with rapid streams all over Britain except East Anglia and south-east England. Is dark brown but looks black, shape like a huge wren with cocked short tail, pure white breast; continually 'bobbing' on stones in water, hence name. Plunges under water and walks on bed to feed on molluscs, etc. Usually one pair to a stretch of stream. Song (heard in almost any month) is loud and clear, accompanying the noise of rushing water. Call, *zit-zit* as it flies up or down stream.

THRUSHES

173. *Mistle thrush:* 11 in. Or Storm Cock, Mistle-toe Thrush. Largest of the family, favours orchards, deciduous woods, some parklands. Much greyer on back than Song thrush, also more boldly speckled. Loud, wild song from tops of tall trees when no other bird singing, and does not repeat phrases like Song thrush. A much wilder bird in every way. Has harsh rattle when alarmed; often found in large flocks in winter.

174. *Fieldfare:* 10 in. Winter visitor from Scandinavia; grey head and rump, chestnut back, dark tail. Feeds in flocks on berried hedgerows, and in fields. Flight call, *chac-chack-chackachak.*

175. *Song thrush:* 9 in. Familiar bird of parks, gardens, orchards and hedgerows everywhere. Light brown back, speckled breast and chuckling call. Song of repeated phrases, *did-he-do-it, did-he-do-it; if he – if he – if he*, etc.

176. *Redwing:* 8½ in. Winter visitor from Scandinavia but now nesting far north Scotland; smallest of family; prominent white eyestripe, streaked breast, reddish flanks and under wings (in flight); very vulnerable in hard winters. Migrates at night, when weak call *see-eep* can be heard overheard in October and November. Has warbling community song (sweeter than starling's) sometimes heard before they leave in spring. Often in fieldfare flocks.

177. *Ring ouzel:* 10 in. Only summer visitor of family; found on wild hills and moorlands, valleys and streams except East Anglia and south-east England. Rather like blackbird but with white crescent on breast; female browner with less defined crescent. Poor singer, repetition of piping notes. Call, *tak-tak.*

178. *Blackbird:* Widespread everywhere, and commonest British breeding bird. All black, yellow bill; female and young speckled brown. Superb singer with fluting notes and rich melodious warblings. Call, loud *pik-pik-pick* on going to roost; also more emphatic *pik-pik* when cat or owl around.

WHEATEAR

179. 6 in. First summer visitor (end March) to open country, hill tops, scree, rocky valleys. Nests in holes, stone walls, etc. Conspicuous white rump, black bar through eye; blue-grey back, black on tail. Brief lark-like warble. Call, *chak-chak-eet*, like two stones knocked together.

STONECHATS

180. *Stonechat:* 5 in. Resident sparingly open heaths, wastes, gorsy cliffs, particularly coastal. Handsome black head, white cheek flash, black wings with narrow white stripe; off-white rump, black tail. Fond of prominent perch, and often gives short, dancing flight. Short song of rapidly repeated notes. Call, *wheet-tak-tak*, like two stones knocked together, hence name.

181. *Whinchat:* 5 in. Summer visitor to commons, open heaths, bracken-covered hillsides, railway cuttings; less coastal than Stonechat; not south-west Ireland. Strongly streaked brown back, light eye-stripe, black cheek patch, buff breast; white flashes on wings and tail. Perches like Stonechat. Song similar to Stonechat. Call, *utik-utik-utiktik*.

REDSTARTS

182. *Redstart:* 5½ in. Also Firebrand-tail. Summer visitor to deciduous woods, parks, old trees, ruins; not Ireland. Black face and throat, conspicuous white forehead, grey head and back, chestnut breast, bright rusty red tail and rump which flashes in courtship and flight. Song robin-like but reedy. Call, *wee-tik-tik*, and an alarm note *weeit* like Willow Warbler and Chaffinch.

183. *Black redstart:* 5½ in. Usually winter visitor but increasingly nesting south-east England and elsewhere in old buildings, ruins, roof-tops, etc. Very dusky brown plumage extending to wings (with white patches); reddish tail, used like redstart's Undistinguished song can be overlooked, being weak and short. Usual call, *tik-tik*.

NIGHTINGALE

184. 6½ in. Summer visitor to south-east England, seldom above Severn-to-Wash line, not Cornwall; occurs rarely south Wales, Yorkshire, Scotland and elsewhere. Sings as much by day as night, usually in good cover where undergrowth affords nesting sites, but skulking and usually solitary. Rusty red plumage with chestnut tail. Song unmistakable with rich *chuk-chuk-chuk* notes, bubbling ones, and *jug-jug-jug*. After young hatched, male has only a croak like a frog.

ROBIN

185. 5½ in. Too well-known to need much description, gardens, coppices, parks, even deep deciduous woods, also city gardens. Bold rather than friendly. Song (10 months of the year) high-pitched but spasmodic with sweet phrases. Call, *tick-tick, tick-tick*.

WARBLERS

Out of the European list of 36 warblers, our list has 13, all except the Dartford warbler being summer visitors, although the Blackcap is found increasingly wintering here. Habitats vary from waterside to woodlands; look out for them on their average arrival dates, as they are then more easily seen when the trees and bushes are only in leaf-bud. Try to learn their songs and notes then, beginning with Chiff-chaff and Willow Warbler (easy to distinguish by voice but not in the field). The waterside warblers (except Grasshopper Warbler) are found in similar sites and their songs and calls need studying – the songs of Reed and Sedge Warblers may at first be confused, but the former has no eye stripe. Two of the most difficult to identify by sound – even to many experienced watchers – are Blackcap and Garden Warbler. Try to *see* them: then there is no possible mistake, but a good Garden Warbler sings nearly as well as a poor Blackcap. Individual birds (of all species) often have individual variations just as human beings have. Compare the songs and calls given under each species below, and make your own interpretations.

186. *Grasshopper warbler:* 5 in. Gorsy commons and heaths, young conifer plantations and rank vegetation. Widespread but not north Scotland. Strongly marked olive-brown upper plumage, somewhat like Dunnock, but lacks blue-grey head and neck of latter. Skulker, but sings from top of bush or small tree, a reeling mechanical-sounding song much like a fisherman's reel being wound in; very high-frequency. Call, *twit-twit.*

187. *Savi's warbler:* 5½ in. Included here because now breeding south-east England in dense reed beds much like commoner Reed and Sedge warblers. Olive-brown above, buff beneath, somewhat like Reed warbler. Song similar to above, but shorter phrases and lower-pitched. Call, *twicktwick* and some ticking notes.

188. *Reed warbler:* 5½ in. Common on riverside and lakeside where *phragmites* reeds abound in continuous stretches, where nest is slung to reed stems. Not Scotland or Ireland. Olive brown back and buffish underparts with no distinctive eyestripe. Climbs up reed stems while singing a loud varied and rapid chatter – *chirruk-chirruk: jag-jag-jag,* etc., often including notes of other birds. Alarm note: a harsh *skirr.*

189. *Marsh warbler:* Very local indeed in thickets, willows and nettlebeds and other dense vegetation, south Midlands and south England only, not Cornwall. Difficult to distinguish from former except by habitat and song: high-pitched, silvery, sometimes canary-like but including many reed warbler notes. Note, *tuc-tuc.*

190. *Sedge warbler:* 5 in. Habitat more varied than Reed Warbler, but usually in thickets and wettish ground, but often in rough farmland borders. Has distinctly 'striped' plumage, underparts creamy, prominent yellowish eye stripe. Often nests close to ground. Song harsher than Reed, not so continuous, rapid repetition of rather grating notes, often mimetic. Call, harsh and churring.

191. *Blackcap:* 5½ in. Woods with good undergrowth, brambles and other bushes in woodland edges; parks where good cover. Grey-brown with lighter underparts; crown black (female's brown); rich song in short stanzas, fluty, liquid and varied; no harsh, scratchy notes; usually sings higher up in trees than next warbler. Call, strong *tac-tac* note.

192. *Garden warbler:* 5½ in. Thickets, commons with plenty of cover; large gardens (often visits soft fruit in season); like Blackcap but lacks distinctive cap. Song less varied than former, longer stanzas but with some scratchy notes (*see* Whitethroat). Similar note to Blackcap.

193. *Whitethroat:* 5½ in. Also Nettle-creeper, Peggy Whitethroat. Bushes, brambles, nettlebeds, gorsy commons. Grey-brown head and back, darker wings. Distinct white throat, prominent in song; white outer-tail feathers. Usually jumps up from top of hedge or bush, singing a distinctly scratchy, unmusical stanza, and quickly returns to perch. Call, harsh *charr*.

194. *Lesser Whitethroat:* 5¼ in. Prefers dense hedgerows and shrubby ground; much greyer than above, with dark splash by eye, not Ireland or Scotland. Often sings from very high up, a rapid 'ching-ching-ching' like beginning of Yellow Hammer's song but more musical, most often from under cover. Call as Whitethroat.

195. *Dartford warbler:* 5 in. Gorsy commons, heather, hillsides with bushes, but now confined to southern England where very scarce; unmistakable, dark brown back, slate grey head, dark chestnut underparts; ruby eye; skulker but sings from top of bush a musical chatter akin to Whitethroat's; call *tuk-tuk*.

93

196. *Willow warbler:* 4¼ in. Widespread in woodland edges, coppices, parks, gardens, etc., with good undergrowth. Olive-greeny-brown, 'pale' legs sings from arrival early April and again before leaving in September, sweet gentle down-the-scale cadence ending on upward note; repeated over and over again; commonest song of summer. Alarm *hweet* similar to Redstart and Chaffinch.

197. *Chiff-chaff:* 4¼ in. Also widespread but more inclined to woodlands; not northern Scotland; colour as above but 'dark' legs in adult. Song a repeated *chip-chap-chep-chip-chap* sometimes with odd guttural notes. Also sings again in September. Has *hweet* note.

198. *Wood warbler:* 5 in. Nearly always in mature oak and beech woods, especially hanging or sloping ones; bright yellow throat, white belly, yellow-green back and wings. Song unmistakable: a stanza that sounds like a coin spun on a metal tray, followed (usually) by *chee-chee-chee* or *dear-dear-dear*.

GOLDCRESTS

199. *Goldcrest:* 3½ in. Smallest European bird, increasing here due to conifer plantations; augmented in winter by Scandinavian birds; stumpy olive-green bird with pale breast; yellow crown edged with black; two thin white bars on wings. Song a very thin, high pitched *wheedly-wheedly-wheedly-weeitt,* rather like wet cork rubbed on windowpane.

200. *Firecrest:* 3½ in. Increasingly recorded in Britain, and same haunts as above, so observation should be careful. *White* stripe over eye and dark stripe *through* eye, same yellow crown. Song said to be lower-pitched than above.

FLYCATCHERS

201. *Spotted flycatcher:* 5½ in. Summer visitor arriving mid-May as a rule; widespread in gardens, lawns, edges of woods, leafy lanes, etc. Brown with grey plumage; very upright stance; lightly-striped throat. Constantly flying up to catch insects and returning to same perch. Poor singer – a few weak *sip-sip-sip-see-see* notes. Call, wee-*tuk-tuk.*

202. *Pied flycatcher:* 5 in. Summer visitor to deciduous woods and parks, similar to redstart, north and west England and east Wales; not eastern England or Scotland. Distinct black and white bird with white forehead and breast; female olive-brown and white. Partial to nest boxes where it breeds. Song variable, *zeeit-zeeit-zeeit* or *tree-pipit, tree-pipit,* followed by trill like Redstart. Call *wee-tick, wee-tick.*

DUNNOCK

203. 6 in. Also Hedge Sparrow, Hedge Accentor, Shuffle-wing. Common resident in gardens, undergrowth, but also coppices and deep lanes. Dark brown streaked back, slate-grey head and neck: very unobtrusive bird that is often seen on lawns picking up trifles when other birds have gone to roost; frequently flicks wings while feeding. Song a thin *wheedly-wheedly-wheedly-weeit.* Call, *see-eek, see-eek.*

PIPITS AND WAGTAILS

204. *Meadow pipit:* 6 in. Resident everywhere, rough ground, meadows, open country, commonest bird on moors and uplands; olive-brown streaked back, streaked breast, white outer-tail feathers. Song: bird rises from ground up to some 15–30 ft., and sings brief tinkling song while parachuting down again. Calls, *pip-it* and *tissit.*

95

205. *Tree pipit:* 6 in. Summer visitor to woodlands, parks and thinly wooded hillsides, not Ireland. Lighter colours than above, yellowish breast. Song starts from top of tree, when bird flies up and utters sweeter song than Meadow pipit, usually ending *seear, seear, seear* and parachuting down to treetop again. Sometimes sings without being airborne. Call *tee-see* and a short *tsip.*

206. *Rock pipit:* 6½ in. Resident on rocky coasts except south-east and eastern England; larger and darker than Meadow pipit; heavily streaked breast, dark legs. Typical pipit-like song, often with flapping flight. Call as Tree pipit.

207. *Pied wagtail:* 7 in. Resident and commonest species: farmland, parks, open country, large gardens. Black and white with long tail continually flicking up and down (smallest bird that *walks*). Is British subspecies of Continental white wagtail, where pied race is scarce, and which has *grey* back with black bib separated from back pattern. Song a brief twitter. Call, *chissik, chissik.*

208. *Grey wagtail:* 7½ in. Resident in same localities as Dipper – hill country with rapid streams. Blue-grey back, black bib, sulphur-yellow breast, longest tail of all wagtails. Undistinguished song; typical wagtail call *chissik,* but higher pitched.

209. *Yellow wagtail:* 6½ in. Summer visitor to England and Wales only; prefers water meadows, rough pastures, especially among cattle. Sulphur-yellow breast, *no* black bib, yellow eyestripe, upper parts yellow-green. Typical wagtail song. Call, *tseep.* (There are races of this species – blue-headed, ashy-headed, grey-headed, black-headed and others: see field guides if in difficulty).

WAXWING

210. 7 in. Winter visitor, sometimes in large numbers, more particularly on eastern coasts. Feeds on berries and has acrobatic habits. Cannot be mistaken: dark cinnamon back and breast; crest a thick tuft over back of head; wing feathers with wax-like red and yellow blobs; distinct yellow band on tail; not a shy bird. Song little known. Call, *shree.*

SHRIKES

211. *Great Grey shrike:* 9½ in. Winter visitor mainly eastern counties but often far inland. Solitary bird with striking grey and white plumage, prominent black eyestripe and black tail and wings, heavy beak. Call, *shek-shek.*

212. *Red-backed shrike:* 7 in. (Or Butcher-bird from habit of impaling young birds, beetles, bees, etc., in 'larder' near nesting site). Summer visitor to southern England, decreasing where formerly common – East Anglia and south-east England. Chestnut back and wings, grey head and rump, black tail, pinkish breast, black eyestripe, heavy bill. Harsh song seldom heard, but has subdued 'warble'. Call, harsh *chak-chak* or *shack-shack.*

STARLING

213. 8½ in. Too familiar to need much description. Gregarious bird with richly speckled winter coat, glossy green and purple plumage in summer, longish pointed bill. Has own clucking and jeering song with wings flapping in time, but imitates other birds such as Curlew, Buzzard, Owls, Poultry, etc., also human whistles. Sings most of year. Huge roosts in winter well worth watching just before sunset. Millions of Continentals augment winter flocks.

D

FINCHES

All finches, buntings and sparrows have thick, seed-eating bills, mostly forked tails, often flock together in winter, and the sexes are usually unalike. They are all resident breeding birds except where otherwise described.

214. *Hawfinch:* 7 in. A resident of orchards, old woods, parklands, etc., but not Scotland, Ireland or western Wales. A very secretive bird as a rule, and easily overlooked, as it is usually silent. Thickset with bullet-head, massive beak (which can crack a cherry stone), large white patch on wing, short tail, general plumage tawny and brown. Flocks in winter often seen feeding on beech mast and especially hornbeam seeds. Twittering song rarely heard. Sharp clicking note – *chip-chip-chip*.

215. *Greenfinch:* 5½ in. Common resident everywhere in open cultivated country, gardens, parks, hedgerows, etc. Olive-green with conspicuous yellow bar on wings, and yellow on sides of tail, both very noticeable in its canary-like flight. Song twittering and easy-flowing, but nearly always interspersed with loud *whee-eeze* or *zree-ee*, which is typical. Call note, *tik-tik-tik*.

216. *Goldfinch:* 4½ in. Or Seven-coloured linnet. Common resident in gardens, orchards, parks, etc. Flocks on thistle patches autumn and winter. Distinctive facial pattern of bright red, black and white; strongly marked black and yellow tail, brown back, bill very pointed. has rather a 'butterfly' flight, and uses tinking notes in the air. Song is also twittering and canary-like (was once a favourite cage-bird). Call, a constant *twit-twit*.

217. *Siskin:* 4½ in. Resident bird common in Scotland and Ireland, and gaining ground elsewhere due to afforestation. Often associated with Redpolls in autumn and winter, when they can both be seen. Strongly marked black cap, yellow and black bars on upper wings; streaked flanks, black tail, yellow rump; rather like small well-marked canary. Song a rapid twitter often with Greenfinch *whee-eeze*. Call, *ty-zizzi* or *sooeat*.

218. *Linnet:* 5 in. Common resident bird everywhere on gorsy heaths, thorny wastes and commons. Forehead and breast carmine, red-brown back (female lacks red); twittering song often uttered from top of bush. Call, *twit-twit*.

219. *Twite:* 5¼ in. Also Mountain linnet. Confined mainly to northern England, Scotland and Ireland, but also found elsewhere in high open country and moorlands, where it breeds. Linnet-like but without red markings, darker wings, pink rump seen in flight, otherwise rich buff streaked with black; bill yellow in winter. Song linnet-like but sharper. Call, *twait*, hence name.

220. *Redpoll:* 5 in. Resident but local over most of Britain in plantations, alders, willows and coppices of mixed woods. Associated in winter with Tits and Siskins in waterside alders. Bright red forehead, short black bib (unlike linnet) very streaked head, back and wings, very forked tail. Song a repeated rippling trill, often in flight, which is very undulating. Call, metallic *tsooee*.

221. *Bullfinch:* 6 in. Resident everywhere in orchards, parks, thickets and dense woodlands. A richly coloured bird with brick-red neck and breast, heavy black head, grey back, black wings with white wing-bar, black tail and white rump very conspicuous in flight. (Our only *resident* finch with this feature, but see Brambling below.) Female more soberly clad, but pairs usually seen together even in winter. Song an indeterminate mixture of wheezy and piping notes, not often uttered. Call (more often heard) a single piping *wheep*.

222. *Crossbill:* 6½ in. Resident and breeding north Scotland and East Anglia, possibly elsewhere, and subject to periodic invasions of Britain (as 1962–63 winter) when they appear in large flocks in coniferous forests, usually mature larch, where they split the cones open for the seeds and can be seen high up the trees with parrot-like poses. Male dull crimson with heavy crossed bill; female olive-green. Rapid undulating flight, when call note *jip-jip-jip* is heard, but often feed silently.

223. *Chaffinch:* 6 in. Commonest finch everywhere from woods to gardens, orchards and farmlands. Fond of nesting in orchards. Bluish head and nape, rufous back, two distinct white wing bars (only resident finch with this feature), breast and underparts dull red. Song vigorous, rapid but monotonous – *tell-tell-tell-cherry-pitee-choo-ee,* usually ending with a flourish. Repeated over and over again from prominent perch. Usual call, *pink-pink* or *spink-spink.* Often associated with following bird in winter flocks.

224. *Brambling:* 6 in. Winter visitor from Scandinavia, often in large flocks. Feeds in beech woods with Chaffinches. Male much more boldly marked than latter, with rich black-brown markings, white rump (diagnostic) and white underparts; breast buffish orange. Female less marked. Song rarely heard here, but has wheezing note like Greenfinch, and harsh *sca-ape* call.

BUNTINGS

225. *Yellow Hammer:* 6½ in. Commonest of all buntings in open country, farm lands, woodland edges, etc., where often seen singing on telephone wires. Lemon-yellow head and underparts, streaked with brown; streaked flanks. Song one of the best-known of all, *a little-bit-of-bread-and-no-o-chee-eese* (often without the latter bit); being much harsher than song of Lesser Whitethroat. Call, *chip-chip-chip.*

226. *Corn bunting:* 7 in. A bulky-looking bird also seen on wires and other conspicuous perches, in open country, farmland, plentiful in eastern England. Reluctant to fly, and dangles legs when it does so. Lacks the yellow of above bird, and is grey-brown streaked with dark brown; heavy beak. Song: a mere jingle, likened to a bunch of keys rattled together. Call, *tsee* and *srip.*

The birds

227. *Cirl bunting:* 6½ in. The scarcest of the buntings, confined mostly to south-west England and south Wales; on cultivated land as two former species, but *very local.* Handsome black-and-yellow facial pattern with blue-black band on neck; black stripe through eye. Back and sides chestnut; breast yellowish with greyish band. Song very like Lesser Whitethroat (*q.v.*) but harsher. Note: *sip* or *siss-sip*.

228. *Reed bunting:* 6 in. Common on rough ground, tussocky patches, wetlands, often in reed beds with Reed and Sedge Warblers. Male very handsome with jet black head and throat, white collar and white stripe up to eye; back dark brown with black streaks; grey-white underparts. Female strongly patterned but lacks black head. Often sings from conspicuous post or reed stem. Song, poorest and briefest of all buntings, a mere *zik-chit-chirry* oft repeated, or *seek-seek-sizzy-sit.* Call, a loud *seek*.

229. *Snow bunting:* 6¼ in. (or Snowflake). Winter visitor in small flocks especially coastal, but breeds sparingly north Scotland. Shows much white especially in flight, which is undulating. Short whistling call, *tsweet*.

SPARROWS

230. *House Sparrow:* 6 in. Common resident everywhere and hardly needs description except to differentiate from next species. Has become a 'parasite' on man, is highest developed species hence place at end of avian evolutionary chain. Grey crown with black bib (female lacks this); slight white streak on wing, dark streaked back and wings; city sparrows extremely dingy and often show no streaks. No real song except grating and chirruping notes.

231. *Tree Sparrow:* 5½ in. Much more local than above; prefers woods, orchards, etc., and is tree-hole nester as a rule but will use tit-boxes which house sparrow cannot enter. Not southern Ireland or Devon and Cornwall. Chestnut head; white cheek with distinct black spot in centre; brighter plumage with more chestnut streaks than House sparrow, with which it seldom associates, often being found in mixed flocks of tits and finches. *Sexes alike.* Call is sparrow-like but much sweeter sounding.

CHAPTER SEVEN

Bird songs and calls

We usually think of the nightingale, blackbird, song thrush, robin and various warblers as our avian 'songsters'. But in talking about bird song we usually think of what pleases the human ear. We would not consider the harsh notes from a rookery or the 'crake-crake' of the land rail as 'song' in the human sense, but there we are judging by our own standards. Whether the song is pleasing or displeasing to our ears, it is all part of the courtship and mating phase, or, in some instances, part of the territorial behaviour pattern, as in the case of our familiar robin, which is one of the very few species that sings for the greater part of the year.

Bird songs and calls are produced by the syrinx, which is the equivalent of the larynx in human beings, and while some bird calls – such as those of the cuckoo and the nuthatch – can be reproduced by the human voice, it is very difficult to imitate most birds, and songs like those of the skylark and reed warbler are beyond the human range, and when attempted appear what they are – imitations.

There used to be, up to the early part of this century, a whole series of what might be called 'mechanical' bird lures and calls, some of them blown into as whistles, while others were used in water to make 'bubbling' calls. There were also some truly 'mechanical' ones, like the wooden cog-wheel with its ratchet, which made a really good imitation of the corn-crake's harsh monotonous call, and several which gave good likenesses of the calls of duck and geese. These lures were used by wildfowlers and others on the marshes to call birds down from the sky, and the writer has seen a curlew brought within close range merely by imitating the flighting call of that bird.

The smaller kinds, which imitated the finches and larks, were used by trappers in a similar way, although equally these gentry often used – and still do so today – live but captive birds in tiny cages, placed close to the decoy traps, so that small flocks of goldfinches or skylarks were attracted to the spot. These mechanical contrivances – and there were very many of them – are quite outmoded today but are well worth buying and preserving if found, as they are not only 'antiques' but interesting relics of a former way of attracting wild birds!

In point of reproduction, these bygones are of course not a match for the wide range of excellent disc recordings that can be obtained everywhere, of which more will be said later. They reproduce the actual voice of the living bird. They are, too, something which the older type of bird watcher never had, and can be used at any time, anywhere, to enable the listener to get to know the difficult species, such as blackcap and garden warbler, or reed and marsh warbler.

It can be said that most birds, large and small, have courtship notes, if not 'songs', and these are used mainly in spring, the breeding season, which may extend from February up to August and September. Indeed, several species, notably yellow hammer and wood pigeon, have an extended breeding season running into very late summer and even beyond, so that there is often a long period when 'song' can be heard. With most species, it is the male only that sings, his purpose being to attract a female down to the territory he has already chosen for the nesting site. That is why, with our summer singers, the warblers, nightingale, redstart and others, the males arrive in the first waves, the females following shortly afterwards.

The purpose of this spring song, therefore, is to lure a partner to the spot, to sing on with a view to eventual mating, nesting and bringing up one or more broods, when the whole purpose of singing has been achieved. In most cases the singing of the male ceases when the young are hatched and both parents are busy from dawn till dusk feeding four or five hungry mouths. There is no time for singing!

The robin is one of the few exceptions in two ways: the female robin sings (and it is quite impossible for us to distinguish the male from the female), and both can be heard well into late autumn and then right through the winter. The reason is that this species is an extremely 'territorial' bird and does not tolerate intruders in his or her well-defined territory*, and this territory is as well guarded in winter as in spring, which is one reason why you never see a 'flock' of robins. His or her song means: 'Keep off the grass!'

But to return to bird song in general, we are very lucky to have in Britain such a wealth of it to enjoy, and this feature of our countryside, parks, gardens and even moors is almost unique. There are several reasons for this. One is that we are still, in spite of all the pressures and changes and development of one kind and another, a 'green and pleasant land', a temperate climate where small birds flourish and are not persecuted, trapped and killed for human food as they are in so many Continental, especially Mediterranean, countries. Then, if you look at the British Isles on a globe, you will see that our tiny islands are an 'oasis' just off the vast European land mass and also off the limitless Atlantic Ocean. This makes Britain an important migration route both in spring and autumn, when countless thousands of birds pass down our coasts and through our country on their way to nesting or winter quarters, where they stay to rest and feed before passing further on, maybe thousands more miles of land and water.

Here, birds are tolerated, with few exceptions. On the Continent, although things are at last on the mend in this respect, birds of *any* species, whether they be thrushes or larks, nightingales or wagtails, are looked upon as just 'more for the pot', and they are trapped literally by the million. Hence bird song on the

*See *The Life of the Robin* by Dr David Lack.

Continent is a mere echo of our own, and although other countries may boast of more species they have not the numbers that would make up a decent dawn chorus as we know it here.

In Britain during the third week in May, when our bird song is at its maximum, in almost any except the wildest, highest parts, where there is reasonable bushy cover, maybe a stream and some deciduous trees, there you can hear the air vibrate with the rich songs of the blackbird (most numerous of all our singers), the many warblers, the resident thrushes and finches, maybe woodpeckers, down to the tiny but loud-voiced wren and the humbler dunnock, all singing their best to greet the rising of the sun. This chorus builds up from early beginnings even in March to reach its maximum at the end of May. As each succeeding week sees new broods hatched or fledged, so the chorus dies away, perhaps imperceptibly, until some time say in mid-June we wake up early in the morning and think how silent it is – not a bird singing, save perhaps a late lark. The whole purpose has been achieved and there will be no more dawn chorus until next spring!

Another reason why we have such a wealth of bird song in Britain is that in most other countries, particularly as we go farther east, there are no true song birds as we know them, the singers there being mostly confined to monotonous pipings and shrieks. Even in the U.S.A. there is no species comparable with our native blackbird, considered by many, including the author, to be our finest consistent singer.

To begin the recognition of bird songs and calls, we must first of all realise that *no two species sing exactly alike*. Even in the case of blackcap and garden warbler, about which some experts disagree, a study of both species reveals subtle differences, and of course individual birds have their own individuality just as human beings have. It is necessary to link up songs with the singers, and this cannot be done in a month or even a season. It is a gradual process of looking and listening, so that one day we realise that we can tell a chaffinch or a whitethroat in song without even seeing the bird. That is the essence of recognition by sound, and it certainly saves an immense amount of time. The author used to cycle long distances at one time, and to be able to recognise a greenfinch or a stock dove without dismounting and without seeing the singer was a great achievement and a time-saver. The reader need not despair if these facilities come but slowly – they *will* come with perseverance, and the results are well worth while.

Begin in mid-winter, when maybe only the great tit is ringing his little bell or calling 'teeteacher, teeteacher'. Link those calls with the bird (although he has many, many more but they are all typical great tit notes and those of no other species). Notice the phrases the robin uses, the sudden burst of wren song from under cover; the calls of the different gulls, mostly herring and black-headed if you live inland; and keep on building up a vocabulary of bird songs and calls, which will keep you busy towards the end of March when the first migrants arrive – wheatear, chiff-chaff, willow warbler, house martin. They will keep you busy but you will win in the end and be able to identify the unseen bird with certainty.

It has been said that it is not easy to 'translate' bird songs into human language; one can only approximate, and often very poorly at that but put *your own* interpretation on what you hear – never mind what so-and-so says in his book. It is your personal opinion that counts – with you!

As already mentioned, 'song' applies mainly to the breeding season, part of a bird's inborn makeup, like nest building and finding its way unaided to winter quarters. The many and varied calls also have their purpose. You will in time be able to recognise anxiety calls, such as when a predator (two- or four-footed) approaches the nesting territory, and there is a certain urgency and warning in such notes. There are flocking calls used by birds such as curlew and peewit, often when they are passing overhead at night, or restlessly roosting in the fields. There are contact notes used by birds that only migrate at night, like the redwing; calls to the newly fledged young when the parent has a beakful of food and is trying to locate the now scattered chicks. There are distress calls, as when an unfortunate bird is the victim of a fox or a bird of prey; sounds that warn all the rest that danger exists. These calls can only be picked up by experience, and the longer you bird-watch the more proficient you will become in recognising bird calls and what they mean. Fortunately, today, there are several excellent discs which faithfully record much of the lesser-known utterances of birds as well as the better-known songs, and these are invaluable aids to successful field work.

Basically, hardly any two species sing and call alike, and experience will reveal to the beginner the differences that arise in the field. If in doubt, try to see the species. There are, too, some 'family' resemblances in songs and calls, as between the various tits, or the finches, and after some experience it will be less difficult to pin down the unseen caller, and to say 'It's either a marsh or a willow tit – let's find the bird!'

Appended to this chapter are two actual dawn-chorus records of bird song, taken down in parkland with ample cover. There is, too, a brief table of song periods of the birds most likely to be met with. This will help in many ways. For instance, if it is singing in July, then it is most unlikely to be a nightingale, but it could be a song thrush. You will notice, too, how the songs of species quickly tail off after the nesting season.

Actual Dawn Chorus Records, taken in two separate years, beginning about 3.30 a.m. in the third week of May, in a habitat of mature woodlands, bushy cover and water :

First Year	*Second Year*
3.45 Pheasant	3.23 Tawny Owl
3.45 Cuckoo (male)	3.27 Lapwing
3.50 Tawny Owl	3.28 Sedge Warbler
3.52 Wood Pigeon	3.30 Waterhen
3.56 Sedge Warbler	3.30 Mallard
4.00 Lapwing	3.35 Heron
4.01 Skylark	3.45 Cuckoo (male)
4.04 Woodcock	3.45 Song Thrush

4.05	Waterhen	3.55	Skylark
4.05	Whitethroat	3.59	Wood Pigeon
4.13	Curlew	3.59	Partridge
4.15	Song Thrush	4.00	Swallow
4.18	Robin	4.01	Robin
4.20	Heron	4.02	Rook
4.21	Garden Warbler	4.03	Blackbird
4.22	Blackbird	4.10	Pheasant
4.22	Carrion Crow	4.11	Garden Warbler
4.26	Dunnock	4.15	Green Woodpecker
4.30	Wren	4.25	Dunnock
4.35	Chiffchaff	4.28	Wren
4.40	Blackcap	4.33	Jackdaw
4.49	Willow Warbler	4.44	Coal Tit
4.50	Rook	4.45	Great Tit
4.51	Tree Creeper	4.46	Little Owl
4.52	Cuckoo (female)	4.49	Chaffinch
4.54	Great Tit	4.55	Tree Pipit
4.55	Goldcrest	4.55	Blue Tit
5.02	Blue Tit	5.00	Chiffchaff
5.05	Green Woodpecker	5.05	Nuthatch
		5.07	Whitethroat
		5.12	Curlew
		5.19	Greenfinch
		5.26	Cuckoo (female)

Total: 29 species

Total: 33 species

Note: The phrase 'Up with the lark' is not borne out by these lists, nor subsequent observations!

There is now a vast choice of disc recordings of bird songs and calls, not only of British species, but from countries all over the world. The voices of our own songsters are to be found on a large array of discs, and the quality of almost every one is first-class. Some of them aim at providing the listener with

	Jan.	Feb.	Mch.	Apl.	May	Jun.	July	Aug.	Sep.	Oct.	Nov.	Dec.
Red Grouse		█	█	█	█	█		█	█			
Corncrake				█	█	█						
Snipe			█	█	█	█						
Curlew			█	█	█	█						
Sandpiper												
Redshank				█	█							
Stock Dove												
Wood Pigeon		█	█	█	█	█	█	█	█			
Turtle Dove					█	█	█					
Collared Dove	█	█	█	█	█	█	█	█	█	█	█	█
Cuckoo				█	█	█						
Tawny Owl	█	█	█	█	█	█				█	█	
Nightjar					█	█	█					
Swift					█	█	█					
Green Woodpecker	█	█	█	█	█	█	█					
Pied Woodpecker		█	█	█	█							
Barred Woodpecker		█	█	█	█							
Wryneck				█	█	█	█					
Woodlark			█	█	█	█						
Skylark	█	█	█	█	█	█				█		
Swallow				█	█	█	█					
Great Tit	█	█	█	█	█	█						█
Blue Tit	█	█	█	█	█	█						
Nuthatch	█	█	█	█	█	█						
Tree Creeper			█	█	█	█						
Wren	█	█	█	█	█	█	█	█		█	█	█
Dipper	█	█	█	█	█	█	█				█	█
Mistle Thrush	█	█	█	█	█	█						
Song Thrush	█	█	█	█	█	█	█					
Ring Ouzel				█	█	█						

	Jan.	Feb.	Mch.	Apl.	May	Jun.	July	Aug.	Sep.	Oct.	Nov.	Dec.
Blackbird		■	■	■	■	■	■					
Wheatear			■	■	■	■						
Stonechat			■	■	■	■	■					
Whinchat				■	■							
Redstart				■	■	■						
Nightingale				■	■							
Robin	■	■	■	■	■	■	■		■	■	■	■
Grasshopper Warbler				■	■	■						
Reed Warbler				■	■	■	■					
Sedge Warbler				■	■	■	■					
Blackcap				■	■	■	■					
Garden Warbler				■	■	■	■					
Whitethroat				■	■	■	■					
Lesser Whitethroat				■	■	■	■					
Willow Warbler			■	■	■	■	■		■			
Chiff-chaff			■	■	■	■	■		■			
Wood Warbler				■	■	■						
Goldcrest		■	■	■	■	■	■					
Spotted Flycatcher					■	■						
Pied Flycatcher				■	■	■						
Dunnock	■	■	■	■	■	■	■			■	■	■
Meadow Pipit			■	■	■	■	■					
Tree Pipit				■	■	■						
Starling	■	■	■	■	■	■	■	■	■	■	■	■
Greenfinch		■	■	■	■	■	■					
Goldfinch				■	■	■						
Linnet				■	■	■	■	■				
Chaffinch			■	■	■	■						
Yellow Hammer			■	■	■	■	■	■				
Corn Bunting			■	■	■	■	■					
Reed Bunting				■	■	■						

practical aids, such as the HMV record XLP 50011, *Guess the Birds*, which is described as 'A new arrangement of bird songs and calls providing entertainment, instruction and a test of skill in aural recognition.' In addition to playing some twenty-four species, it has a comprehensive folder to be read while the record is playing and an arrangement, whereby, after one has heard the preliminary section, these birds are 'scrambled' and the listener is asked to put down his or her answer to the now unannounced singers and callers. This is excellent practice.

Some other readily available discs are as follows:

Tapestry of Bird Song: HMV CLP 1723

Bird Recognition: HMV 3 vols: 7EG 8923–26–29

Bird Sounds in Close-up: (Victor Lewis): Marble Arch 1102, Vol. 1

Bird Sounds in Close-up: (Victor Lewis): Marble Arch 1316, Vol. 2

Wild Life in Wales: BBC Wildlife Series (there are others) RED96M. Discourses, 10a High Street, Tunbridge Wells, publish a comprehensive list of recordings ranging from eighteen 7 in. $33\frac{1}{3}$ discs of all the common and lesser-known species; bird concerts, birds musicians, and the 'Shell' series. The RSPB, The Lodge, Sandy, Bedfordshire, has a wide choice, sold separately or in sets, and Witherby's *Sound Guide to British Birds* consisting of two 12 in. $33\frac{1}{3}$ discs and a book on identification. A detailed catalogue is obtainable.

For indoor use and to familiarise oneself with bird songs and calls, or indeed to confirm some unknown species heard in the field, these recordings are exceptionally useful. They can of course be played over and over again, and are particularly useful to groups of young bird watchers. All the above discs are 'mono' but can be played on stereo apparatus; we have been promised stereo bird recordings for some time; up to the time of writing they have not seen the light of day!

CHAPTER EIGHT

Birds in the garden

When one reads that every eight years an area of land the size of Nottinghamshire disappears under bricks and mortar, and that, increasingly, all kinds of land and water are undergoing pressures of many kinds – building, industry, recreation, to name but a few – it can be appreciated that all wild life, including our wild birds, must be affected by the drastic changes that are taking place at an ever-increasing pace. Where woods are felled and factories built the avian population is the first to suffer. Indeed, as regards pollution, both of land and water, and the increasing use of pesticides, insecticides and fungicides in agriculture and horticulture, and of chemicals in industrial processing, birds are the early warning system that tells us that the effects on wild life will eventually reach man.

The new threats to the far north of Scotland – not only on the eastern side but later on the western side – from oil and gas exploitation of the seas around us, will, we are told, eventually 'transform the landscape'. If that is so, bird life in those wild and remote places will be the first to be affected seriously. Birds were here millions of years before man – the most destructive creature ever placed on earth – arrived, and surely our native songsters and our handsome woodpeckers and the kingfisher, together with our robins and swallows and all the other wild species, deserve some consideration.

In any case, they, like us, are part and parcel of the complicated pattern of life we call the 'balance of nature', and on the whole and in the long run, their activities benefit man. But what has all this to do with birds in the garden, it may be asked. The fact is that our gardens, however small and urbanised, can become bird reserves and help to counterbalance the threats that are ever present and even increasing in our countryside, however remote it may seem.

All our smaller garden birds, even the house sparrow, which has a breeding season often extending over three months, feed their young broods (often two or more) on insects, grubs, caterpillars and other pests of soil and crops, and it is up to us to encourage their beneficial activities. Blue tits have often been accused of eating our garden peas, on the circumstantial evidence of their having been caught searching the pea rows diligently. In fact, these birds have actually been shot 'in the act', but no trace of vegetable matter was found in their bodies. What they were after were the maggots that often infest the pods.

Bullfinches are – often rightly – blamed for the destruction of fruit buds. This damage most often occurs in the spring, and is more prevalent when one of the natural wild foods of this bird, the ash keys, fails, as it does every few years, resulting in an invasion of the commercial orchards in fruit-growing areas. The trouble can be minimised by putting out drinking water in suitable spots, but in these days of modern methods of growing large acreages of soft fruits it is natural that insect pests, as well as bullfinches, 'benefit' from man's activities. Blackbirds are fond of strawberries; efficient netting will usually take care of this. But there is no need to feed the birds all the year round, and you may be quite sure that your efforts in this respect will not result in an invasion of bullfinches!

Only in the winter months, from October to March, is it advisable or necessary to tide birds over a hard period. Peanuts, wild bird foods, kitchen scraps, bacon and cheese rinds, all can be put out, together with drinking water, which is important and overlooked. But there is a right and a wrong way of putting food out.

A bird table should be a *safe* place for our friends to feed on. Ideally, it is a plain board on a *tubular* post. The 'rustic' type of table, with maybe a thatched roof, or ye olde Tudor cottage, is no more attractive to the birds than the plainest, and there is no need for a roof or canopy either. Many species like thrushes do not like feeding under cover unless they are very hard pressed. Cats and grey squirrels, and maybe rats, can climb up the wooden post – and many people would be surprised at the four-footed creatures that prowl round their gardens and lawns at night! There is a sound reason for placing food on the table and not on the path or lawn. True, some species like song thrush, dunnock and chaffinch, dislike landing on even the open table, but a similar board placed on the ground will cater for these rather choosy species, and the board can be taken up at dusk and placed in shed or garage out of the way of nocturnal prowlers.

Half coconuts can be suspended by hooks from the table – but *never* put out desiccated coconut as this is one of the most dangerous foods for wild birds. Sunflower heads will attract greenfinches, goldfinches and others. Hawthorn trees, cotoneasters and other berried bushes will be popular with many species, and in a favourable winter waxwings will delight with their beautiful plumage and confiding ways.

If the garden is large and surrounded by more or less 'open' country or woodlands, or if you have a bit of 'rough' ground or a small orchard, then you are indeed lucky and may attract the pied woodpecker, nuthatch, and maybe marsh and willow tits. But do not despair if it is not much more than a suburban 'cabbage patch'. Apart from the inevitable sparrows and starlings, and possibly pigeons, blue tits and chaffinches can be attracted, and often some stray 'rarity' will bring a red-letter day.

Another way of not only attracting birds but affording much pleasure to others, is to have a window-sill table (quite easy to make) to a ground-floor room or even a bedroom window, where a house-bound person can enjoy the birds. When the birds get used to approaching so closely to the house, the number of species will increase, and unending delight will be given to the watch'er.

At the end of March, unless there is a harsh weather patch, feeding should stop except perhaps for household scraps placed on the table. It is entirely wrong to put food out all summer; it encourages nesting birds to become lazy and to take the most easily available food and some food, like peanuts, could be fatal to young birds. Their natural food in the breeding season is as previously stated, and this is found increasingly in and around gardens. That's why, for instance, tits and other youngsters are around when the trees are often covered with tiny caterpillars – Nature times the food supply to meet the ravenous needs of the young.

Mid-winter is a good time to put up nesting boxes in suitable places, to attract tits, robins and other desirable residents in the early spring. Once again, do not be misled into thinking that the nest box must be "attractive' to the birds. They are not in the least aesthetically-minded, and experience has shown that often the rougher and less finished the box is, the better success it may have.

If you are lucky enough to have, say, four well-grown trees, do not overcrowd the place by putting up a box on each one. Space them out and put two boxes only on them, as far apart as possible. Others may be fixed to wall, shed or garage, but they must all be high enough to be out of the easy reach of cats; grey squirrels you will never counter unless they are eliminated, and they are real enemies to all birds, their eggs and young. Eight to ten feet should be the minimum height, and a box should *never* be placed with the entrance facing the sun, i.e. south or west. The sun shining into a box in such a position can be fatal to nestlings. In a 'natural' hole site, in a tree limb or trunk, the material is 'solid' and the inside temperature seldom varies, whichever way the hole faces. Always, therefore, place the box facing between east and north, and when possible sloping slightly to the front so that it is protected from heavy rain.

Birds in the garden

A nest box can often be erected where it is visible from the house, thus affording increased pleasure and interest. With such a box one can time the feeding visits and thus calculate the amount of food – caterpillars, grubs, insects, etc., taken in.

Commercial boxes of good type can be purchased, but they should comply with certain minimum requirements and be adequate in depth and capacity. A box can be too small or too shallow, but seldom too deep, and the entrance hole must not be too large, although this depends on the species you wish to encourage. If your commercial box has a perch outside, cut it off, or sparrows might use it to keep out the rightful tenants, even if the hole is too small for them to get in! Generally speaking, to encourage both great and blue tits, the hole must not exceed $1\frac{1}{8}$ in. diameter (that of a 10p piece).

It is quite easy to make one's own nest boxes, and they can be made out of the roughest type of wood available. The diagram shows how a simple type of nest box can be made from a 40 in. length of wood, plus a piece for the roof. The dimensions given should be taken as minimum. If, however, you are able to attract either a nuthatch or a pied woodpecker, a larger hole is necessary, but then there is always the risk of sparrows or starlings occupying the box.

An 'open' type of nest box (*see diagram*) will attract a robin, maybe a spotted flycatcher, or at least a blackbird, and this type of box should also face away from the sun as far as possible.

At the end of the season, when your birds have flown (and they will not come back to the box again that season), you should clear the boxes out. Not only do old nest contain parasites that quite *naturally* live on the wild birds (see the note on this in our final chapter), but they often hibernate until next nesting season! You may find, too, that many nest boxes will be used as winter roosts, often by more than one species. Wrens are particularly fond of using them in this way.

One can learn a great deal about the behaviour of garden birds merely by watching. Notice how ravenously the starlings fall on the food put out – could it be their metabolism is

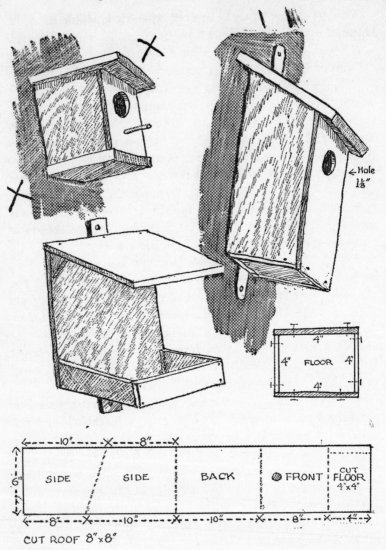

There are *six* things wrong with the nest box on upper left: Can you spot them? See foot of p. 120 for answers

similar to that of the mole, who must be constantly feeding or die? In contrast note how leisurely the song thrush approaches food, be it kitchen tit-bits or a juicy snail put down on the lawn on purpose. There is no hurry – all the time in the world to feed. The author has known a thrush take ten minutes to reconnoitre and finally take away a snail to its rocky 'anvil'. The industrious 'after-hours' feeding of the dunnock is very noticeable, and a lesson in 'waste-not, want-not'; no crumb is left, and they prefer to pick up all the unconsidered trifles when all the rest have gone to their roosting quarters.

The acrobatics of tits and goldfinches are always worth watching, and although the former will take away a peanut and grasp it in their claws to peck at, no other species has the same 'sense'. Then, too, blue tit and great tit will feed on or near the spot; but not so the coal tit (sometimes a very casual visitor to the table) which often takes the nut away and hides it in crevices in walls and rockeries, probably never to find it again!

The photography of birds at nest boxes and feeding devices is dealt with in chapter ten, and examples of this kind of work are also given. The ingenuity of the photographer is called for here; without disturbing the sitting bird, the work can be carried out in private and comfortable conditions within familiar surroundings.

One final point about birds – and other creatures – in the garden. The growing use of pesticides, insecticides and herbicides in gardens is giving rise to much concern. The organochlorines – D.D.T., B.H.C., Dieldrin, Aldrin, Heptachlor, Lindane and Chlordane, to name a few, have been found in the bodies of birds found dead in gardens, especially those adjacent to fields where crops are sprayed. These chemicals, or any proprietary brands which contain them, must NOT be used, otherwise birds and other creatures will be endangered. The safest types of sprays are made from pyrethrum and derris, both harmless to wild life. Many weed killers, too, can indirectly kill birds; see that they do not contaminate drinking water or bird baths or garden ponds. In all cases, such chemicals must be used as directed, when they will cause a minimum of damage. If any chemicals are used to excess, the very pests we wish to

Beginner's Guide to Bird Watching

destroy will in time develop resistance, thus starting all over again the deadly circle of poisons in increasingly lethal forms.

Further reading:
Birds in a Garden Sanctuary Staples, Warne, 1946
Bird Gardening Maxwell Knight, Routledge, 1954
(These two books are long out-of-print but are often obtainable in libraries, and sometimes in second-hand bookshops.)
The Bird Table Book Tony Soper, Pan Books
Nestboxes Flegg & Glue, 30p
The Nest Record Scheme Mayer-Cross, 40p
(The last two are available from the British Trust for Ornithology, whose address is on p. 170.)

Answers to Diagram 2 on p. 118.
The nest-box shown is:
(i) Too shallow; hole-nesting birds like tits will prematurely 'explode' from such a box. The young need to jump inside the box until they are ready for 'off'.
(ii) The roof should slope towards the front, or tilt the box forward.
(iii) The hole is too big and will admit sparrows; $1\frac{1}{8}$ in. is ample for tits.
(iv) A perch must not be fixed, otherwise sparrows will keep others out.
(v) The floor should be *inside* the walls, otherwise rain will soak in and make the nest damp. (Natural hole nests are in solid wood.)
(vi) The box should be fixed so that it slopes somewhat towards the front, allowing rain to run off quickly.

CHAPTER NINE

Bird migration and ringing

Why do some birds migrate while others stay here more or less all the year round? Why do most warblers, insectivorous birds, leave us entirely in the winter, yet both the blackcap and garden warbler, also entirely insectivorous, leave some of their numbers to winter here? Why is the Darford warbler the only true warbler which is resident here the whole year round and suffers for it accordingly during hard weather? Why are young robins, usually regarded as resident birds, bred in Britain, sometimes recovered from France and the Pyrenees? And how do migrating birds find their way? The truth is that much of the entire story of migration still remains a mystery. Many species, like the swift, leave us when the insect population is still at its height!

A favourite theory of the past was that the glacial epochs, the advance and retreats of the ice-caps, caused the wild creatures to advance and retreat accordingly, but as these epochs occupied tens of thousands of years, this theory no longer holds good, as bird migration is an annual event . . . but is it? There is no month in the year in which migration of some kind does not take place, as ringing and the observations of amateur ornithologists have proved. True, the peak periods are spring and autumn, but there is movement of birds in every month. There is, indeed, much more to be learned of this vast and fascinating subject, and it is an exercise in which every one of us can play a part, however small. Records of the arrival of our summer and winter visitors are fairly easy to achieve; it is much more difficult to record their departure, because then they are normally silent.

Gilbert White, whose classic *The Natural History of Selborne* was the pioneer book of the true field naturalist (and which has been translated into no less than sixty languages), was perhaps the first serious student of the habits and classification of our common birds, – and indeed was the first person to separate the three 'leaf' warblers – chiff-chaff, willow warbler and wood warbler – believed quite seriously that such birds as swallows and martins buried themselves in the mud banks of rivers in the autumn! It was, in medieval times, thought that birds journeyed to the moon and that migration took place at tremendous heights, simply because astronomers, aiming their telescopes at the moon and planets, actually saw flocks of migrants passing across their vision. They certainly did, but not at such heights and for such distances as they supposed!

It is now largely accepted that birds 'navigate' by the sun and stars, and have something inborn in them that enables them to find their way, sometimes over thousands of miles, unerringly, to and from their place of birth. Homing pigeons certainly do this, and there is no reason why our migratory species should not do the same thing. Certainly the 'urge' to migrate is strong at the proper season. So strong, indeed, that house martins and swallows, having very late broods, will often abandon the nestlings to their fate – death very quickly overtakes those that have been denied food for even a few hours – and wing their way to Africa when the overwhelming instinct or whatever it is compels them to start on their hazardous journeys.

But, like man, the bird gets confused and lost in fog and bad weather, which is why tens of thousands are found dead at the foot of and around our lighthouses during such weather conditions. Steps have been taken to minimise this by placing perches around the lantern or the catwalk, and more recently by floodlighting the whole structure of the lighthouse from below, which does not affect the navigational beams but enables thousands of birds to avoid the place altogether.

It is only since the advent of bird ringing – banding as our American friends have it – that we have been able to find out not only about the routes and time taken by migrants, but also how long they live, with some surprising results. The first recorded ringing of birds was probably the Northumbrian one in 1890 when some young Woodcock were ringed. In 1909 the magazine *British Birds*, in conjunction with Dr J. Landsborough Thompson, did the first really serious ringing of wild birds, and since then the project has grown to be international. Thousands of ringers all over the world ring, weigh and record their captures, exchange information, and have their operations collected and collated so that we now have a vast amount of material of great importance to science and the everyday bird watcher. Almost every county has its band of ringers and there are bird observatories dotted all around our coasts and in many inland places, too, where this study is pursued mostly by spare-time and week-end enthusiasts.

Today the would-be ringer has to be apprenticed to a fully qualified ringer for two years to learn the technique, not only of handling the bird correctly so that no harm is caused, but also to be able to identify the species unmistakably, and to fill in approved records for submission to the central authority. In this country this is the British Trust for Ornithology, Beech Grove, Tring, Hertfordshire, although many of the older records bear the name of the British Museum. Rings, of different sizes and of an approved pattern, are issued only to qualified ringers, and they bear a serial number so that every used ring has to be accounted for – and paid for – by the ringer. Rings are fitted to the left leg (usually), and have to be fitted loosely with a special type of pliers so that no injury is likely to be sustained.

Whenever a bird has been recovered, either dead or re-trapped somewhere, or shot or otherwise found, the details on the ring are sent to the address given on it, so that the central record office can link it up with the original ringer, who is notified of the recovery. The finder, too, is told who ringed the bird and when and where. By this means a remarkably world-wide record is being built up. But of course not all rings are recovered. In the case of the smaller birds such as warblers or swallows, the return rate is very small, about 2 per cent, but when tens of thousands of these birds are ringed annually, these returns give a good picture of the movements and longevity of species. In the larger birds, such as gulls and ducks, the recovery rate is of course much larger. Detailed location maps are kept at all bird observatories and ringing centres, and even to the local ringers they reveal some interesting facts.

It is not unusual for birds such as starlings to be recovered near Moscow; for chaffinches to be 'controlled' – i.e. picked up again – at ringing stations, in Scandinavia. The majority of recoveries of small migrants are around the coasts of France and Spain, Portugal and across the Straits of Gibraltar, proving that, contrary to the older surmises that migrating birds went straight across the sea, they follow more or less a coastal route. So they avoid the risks involved in large stretches of open sea, and it enables them to come down, if necessary, for rest and recuperation, on dry land. Accidents happen, of course, and thousands of migrants are blown out of course by adverse wind conditions – which neither they nor we can forecast! – and sudden squalls upset the courses which migrants have followed for tens of thousands of years.

In 1927 – and again much more recently – a flock of lapwings or peewits, normally a partially migratory species in this country, driven by a 55 m.p.h. gale, was blown across the Atlantic to Newfoundland, 2,200 miles away, where this species had not been previously recorded! As it happened, one of the flock had been ringed as a nestling in Cumberland, so the hazardous freak migration of these birds was proved. How many of the flock had perished in the ocean we do not know. It is not so unusual in these days of ringing for South American species, such as some of the rare waders or Wilson's phalarope, to occur in Britain when the winds are south-westerly. Indeed, bird ringing is full of surprises, as well as teaching us much about the lives and movements of wild birds.

Experiments have been carried out from time to time to ascertain the capabilities of bird to return to their breeding haunts. Shearwaters, a purely pelagic species, which nest in thousands off the south Welsh coasts but which is not normally a 'European' bird except in different species, and which seldom appear in daylight, were taken from their burrows, crated and taken to Venice by air, where they were released. Within fourteen days some of those birds were back at their nests, having flown, as the proverbial crow flies, 930 miles, or 3,700 miles by the normal migratory routes through the Mediterranean! Swallows, nesting at Bremen in Germany were taken by air to Croydon and released. The first birds were back at their nests within four days! Can these remarkable feats of navigation be explained, except by the fact that birds have some inborn faculties which man has never possessed?

Another fact brought out by ringing is the life expectancy of birds. Dr David Lack, in *The Life of the Robin,* states, after a lifetime studying the small birds, that the *average* life of such birds is 13.3 months, and that of a song thrush or starling about a year and a half; a lapwing or blackheaded gull two and a half years. These may seem unbelievable figures, but the truth is that these and other small birds often have two or more broods of, say, four or five young at a time, yet at the end of a season we cannot say that there is any noticeable increase in the numbers of robins. Small birds in particular are subject to enormous risks in the nestling and fledgeling stages – from predation, disease, accident and other causes – otherwise, as Dr Lack suggests, 'If the average life were appreciably longer and the replacement rate remained the same, Britain's robins would increase so rapidly as to become a plague.' But there are notable exceptions to these general rules. A swallow ringed in Ross-shire, Scotland, in 1911 was killed by a cat in 1920. Since then, one ringed at Cley, Nortolk, in 1935 was recovered at the same place in 1961, a total life of sixteen years – and an estimated migrational travel of 190,000 miles, excluding its home life!

Incidentally, the pattern of migration of swallows can be seen on a map in Dr Landsborough Thompson's work *Bird Migration*. This shows us that these birds usually arrive in Gibraltar and similar latitudes in mid-February; in southern France mid-March; in England early April; Scotland late April; Scandinavia mid-May and north Norway (their farthest northern limits) in early June. There is thus a process of 'leap-frogging', migrants for stations farther north going on over the heads of the birds already established in more southerly climes. Again speaking of swallows, or fifty-nine birds recovered in successive years after ringing, most were found in or around old nesting sites. The farmer who tells you he has had the same swallows nesting in his barn for eighteen years running is only partly right – for the descendants of the original birds will have returned from subsequent broods. Most swallows – and many other species – return to breed in or around old nesting sites. Many have been found, through ringing nestlings, within a dozen miles of their parental nest; some are found up to 100 miles from their birthplace.

The distance covered by migrants is also becoming clearer through ringing recoveries. We know that swifts cover about 6,000 miles each way in their journeys to and from South Africa, and remember they live on the wing too in this country! The goldcrest, our smallest species, which arrives here in autumn from Scandinavia in large numbers, crosses the North Sea in a single night, a journey of 400–450 miles – non-stop! Humming birds, too, regularly cross the Gulf of Mexico, a distance of 500 miles, in one hop. Arctic terns, which have the longest migrational journey of any bird, flying from the Arctic Circle to the Antarctic, cover 11,000 miles, estimated at 1,000 miles a week. Penguins, too, 'migrate' from one zone to another, either by swimming, or even sliding along ice and snow on their tummies!

Bird migration and ringing

A lot of vague and unreliable figures as to the speeds at which birds fly have been given from time to time, but with air travel and radar we are beginning to know something not only of the speeds, but the heights which they achieve. Storks are known to fly at some 4,200 ft. on migration; swifts have been encountered at 5,000 ft., while smaller birds fly at anything from a few hundred to between two and three thousand feet. Although the peregrine falcon may touch 60 m.p.h. in 'stooping' to its pigeon or duck prey, and the swift may touch this when pursued by a hobby, the most reliable records we have at present give small birds – finches, warblers, larks, etc., a speed of 20–37 m.p.h., crows a speed of 21–45 m.p.h., and ducks 44–69 m.p.h.

All birds preparing to migrate 'feed up' prior to the journey, in some cases doubling their normal weight. That is why regular weighing at ringing stations is part of the procedure; if a bird is heavier than normal it is probably migrating; if it is the normal weight of the species, it is a local resident bird. It is estimated that a swift requires some 20,000 insects a day to sustain health, and a meal may consist of anything from 300 to 1,000, probably mostly aphides which swarm in the upper air, and which are caught by the swift in its remarkable large gape, on the wing.

So, from all the facts and figures given in this chapter, the reader will appreciate what a vast and fascinating subject migration can be. We by no means know all the answers.

Many waders pass down our eastern coasts and through sewage farms in mid-August. From their plumage, one can tell these are young birds which only hatched some four or six weeks before! In that short time they have fully fledged, and have the inborn instinct that enables them to fly from within the Arctic Circle to our shores, from whence they depart south, past the Equator into the southern hemisphere. Next spring they return by the same route back to the Arctic. Ringing has proved that, but it does not give us the answers as to *why* or *how* the birds migrate!

Further Reading:
Down the Long Wind Garth Christian Newnes, 1961
Bird Migration J. Landsborough Thompson, H. & F. C. Witherby, 1942

CHAPTER TEN

Bird photography

'You must have a very good camera' or 'a very good lens' is a common remark made when one secures, either by hard work or a fluke, an outstanding photograph. That is no compliment to the photographer, however. Just as a range of expensive artists' colours and the most costly brushes do not make a competent painter, neither does a camera body costing perhaps £200, plus a multiplicity of expensive gadgets and telephoto lenses necessarily turn out a good photographer. It is the person behind the camera that counts, the brain that composes and produces the picture, and that goes for the simplest apparatus or the most expensive. Prize prints have been achieved with Box Brownies! The secret is knowing the possibilities – and limitations – of your equipment and being able to utilize it to the utmost. There is no ideal camera that will do every type of job from ultra close-ups to long-distance views, unless one contemplates buying a mass of accessories. Optically, too, it is not possible to fit what many people call 'telescopic lenses' to the simple pocket camera with a 'fixed' lens.

This chapter does not pretend to teach the would-be photographer the technicalities of processing, printing, enlarging – there are literally scores of books in your local library which will give you all the information you require on these subjects, and your local dealer will be only too pleased to help and guide you to better pictures. One of the ambitions of almost every young bird photographer is to emulate the achievements of the

Keartons, Oliver Pike, Arthur Brook, G. K. Yeates, Eric Hosking and a host of others who have in their time reached the pinnacles in the art of bird photography, first in monochrome as the pioneers did, and later in glorious colour. But we must learn to walk before we can run.

Books on birds, illustrated with superb examples of the photographers' work, are legion, and the best can be studied in libraries (or borrowed), and frequently appear on the second-hand shelves at reasonable prices. But books devoted solely to the art of bird photography are comparatively few and mostly out-of-print. Every one of the outstanding photographers began with the simplest of cameras and worked their way up, so to speak, to the modern interchangeable-lens camera and later the ciné camera plus sound.

In the early days of bird photography, which were the closing years of the nineteenth century, there were few rules based on experience to be followed, and unfortunately, in many cases, the welfare of the bird was the last consideration that mattered – they had not heard of protection and conservation in those far-off days. Even in recent years much criticism has been directed at those who made the making of a 'picture' the be-all and end-all of the matter. The author has seen good work by experienced photographers who have obviously done their 'gardening' only too well. Reeds cut with scissors in front of a nest to let in the light and avoid out-of-focus vegetation; branches sawn from trees so that the nest and feeding parents could be more successfully *exposed* (that is surely the right word!). Inevitably, just as people's tracks to a well-known nest site betray the whereabouts of the birds, however well-concealed, to both natural and human predators, so too the inevitable jay, magpie, grey squirrel, rat or cat finds the fully exposed nest; the result is inevitable destruction.

If a hide is used at a nest site, it is essential that it be erected some distance away and moved gradually up to within camera range. This can only be done a little at a time, and may take a week or more; in the meantime no anxiety should be caused to the sitting bird. It is a good idea to take a companion, who can leave the site ostentatiously, and return when required at a pre-arranged signal such as a handkerchief pushed out at the back of the hide. Drastic 'gardening' at the nest site is not only unnecessary but highly undesirable. Foliage should be *tied back unobtrusively* and temporarily, and must be replaced as quickly as possible and all traces of the photographer's presence obliterated – trampled grass brushed up, footprints wiped out, etc. If it is impossible to get pictures without cutting away tree branches or otherwise exposing the nest, then no attempt at all should be made. The author has rarely used a hide, preferring the 'remote control' technique which, while limiting the number of pictures possible, means security for the birds. Nesting birds have enough enemies without adding unnaturally to their number. There are ways and means of photographing wild birds – and other creatures – at home without causing disasters to the nestlings or even causing the parents to desert, which they will do if interference is too persistent to be tolerated.

Fortunately the law can be invoked in some circumstances to protect certain species, and while we need not assume that photography is 'illegal', under the Wild Birds Protection Acts 1954 to 1967 if one wishes to take photographs of scheduled species, a permit to do so must be applied for from the Department of the Environment, and this is not readily granted. The applicant has to furnish proof of his or her capabilities and experience, and give references to those who can vouch for the integrity of the would-be photographer. Unnecessary disturbance of sitting birds or their young is now an offence (*See* Appendix I). But there is much that can be done without breaking the law and without causing harm.

It is, and has already been said, the person behind the camera that counts, and the choice of apparatus is only limited by the purse and ambition of the photographer. Modest apparatus, provided its limitations are appreciated, is no bar to good results. The author began with a simple folding $\frac{1}{4}$-plate camera which took glass plates and had a very simple lens and a two-speed shutter! It cost, *new*, 17s. 6d! Exposures had to be guessed in those days of slow materials, but a little under- or over-exposure was neither here nor there, as it could be easily adjusted in the subsequent developing and printing process.

Progress continued through the simple box film camera to the folding pattern, the heavy but efficient 'reflex' camera where one saw the actual image, right away up, on a clever mirror arrangement which swung out of sight the moment one pressed the shutter. Great strides have taken place in apparatus and techniques ever since the pioneer days, and the camera has become *almost* automatic, but not quite. One can use a camera that has a built-in exposure meter, will tell you when it is not suitable to take a photograph, and so on; but none of these costly and elaborate pieces of mechanism will enable you to turn out masterpieces, or even good photographs, time after time. The eye and brain are still needed to compose and select the subject; the psychological moment when to press the shutter is still yours!

If you have a simple box camera – a type that is now very 'dated' in view of the modern 'instamatic' and comparatively cheap camera – you can still take photographs of *large* nests and eggs, up to not less than three feet from the subject. If you go nearer the result will be blurred, due to the fact that this type of camera has an extremely simple 'single' lens and shutter, which have only limited uses in a 'snapshot' camera, which, after all, this type of instrument is. It is not usually possible to attach 'close-up' lenses to it, in order to get closer to the subject; for one thing you cannot see in the view-finder how the closer viewpoint affects the clarity of the picture on the film.

The next type is the older 'folding' camera, which usually takes a film going under the number of 127 or 120. This is a big improvement on the box-type, which will sometimes take what are called supplementary lenses, but here we are still up against the fact that you cannot see the effect of these lenses on your film base, and the distance between lens front and subject has to be accurately measured according to the scale provided with the diopter lenses, as they are called. Results with either of the two types of camera just mentioned, when one attempts to photograph birds themselves, will inevitably be disappointing. People often go out into the garden to picture some 'tame' blackbird or even a robin, only to find that, although the resulting picture may be correctly exposed and in focus, the subject is 'tiny'. One can therefore rule out such cameras for serious work.

There is a bewildering range of photographic apparatus of all kinds on the market today, costing from a very few pounds to many hundreds. But there is no 'specialist' type of camera made for the would-be bird photographer. He, or she, has to either accept the recommendation of an experienced friend, or take a chance and experiment with what may be thought to be the nearest camera to an ideal one. The author has tried every type on the market, both still and ciné, from the simplest to some which are admittedly rather complicated for the beginner, but he has never owned a camera that cost more than £40; indeed, much of the work done on birds has been with such a straightforward instrument as the Silette – although any equivalent make of the same type would do equally well. The present-day popularity of the 35 mm camera (an idea described not so many years ago as a 'passing fad'!) has become almost universal, although the twin-lens reflex taking a $2\frac{1}{4}$ in. square picture with a full-size viewing lens incorporated, has big advantages for the black-and-white user. Colour in such a size tends to be expensive.

The coming of the single-lens reflex 35 mm type, with which one can focus directly 'through the lens', is probably the one best suited and most likely to give uniformly good results to the amateur bird photographer. Indeed, the professionals of today use this kind regularly, although of course they keep abreast of all the modern developments in this respect. It has, too, the advantage of interchangeable lenses, so that one can enjoy the choice of ultra close-up, telephoto and other types, including extension rings to enable photo-micrography to be attempted.

A word about these specialised lenses may not come amiss

here. One sees attractive advertisements of telephoto (including 'zoom') lenses, ranging from the modest 135 mm to 'long toms' up to 400 mm, which seems at present to be the ultimate range, in other words they will bring a far distant subject within range of your miniature camera, which is literally screwed on to the end of the long lens! But there is a snag with these higher-powered 'guns' – the more powerful the less the depth of field at long distance. That is to say, one has to be dead accurate with focusing, as the subject is in a narrow band with out-of-focus material in front and behind it. With the single-lens reflex camera this is of course taken care of, but with moving birds, especially in flight, one has to have great experience to be able to be confident of good, crisp results.

For moving subjects it is better to rely on the less powerful lenses where the depth of focus is very much deeper and there is a better chance of success. Nevertheless the telephoto lens can be used in another way. Suppose one wants to picture garden birds, at, say 8 ft. or 9 ft. distant. The 135 mm lens comes in very well here, and in addition to a sharp picture the background is thrown completely out of focus, thus providing a model that seems to stand out from the surroundings. But with any kind of telephoto lens it is advisable, if not absolutely essential, to use a firm tripod or other steady support, otherwise the complaint of 'camera-shake' will be prevalent. Many photographers advise – and so do the books – that whatever the lens or camera, the slowest speed that can be 'hand-used' is 1/125th sec.

Whether the telephoto lens can be left to a later date, when the would-be photographer has had some experience and some expert advice, is a debatable point, but there is no doubt about the exposure meter. This is, with today's comparatively high-speed film material, a necessity. Whether it is incorporated within the camera body, as many are in the latest models, or whether one relies on the separate instrument – and there are many very reliable ones on the market – is a matter of choice and pocket. In the past it might not have mattered very much, as with the slower kinds of black-and-white material one could intensify or reduce one's negatives in the processing. But the higher the speed of film stock used, the more accurate the exposure has to be.

The tripod has been mentioned before. This is an essential for heavy supplementary lenses, and also for hide work. It should be substantial, either of metal or wood, with the added accessory of a pan-and-tilt head, which enables the camera to be put at any angle necessary for photography.

One of the most valuable bits of apparatus, which has been largely used by the author to secure many of the pictures included in this book, is a 'remote control'. This can be an electrically operated one which is rather expensive, but the simplest and most foolproof kind is the pneumatic type, operated with a bulb, very much like the old-fashioned 'watch the birdie' kind that the studio photographer used. It is readily available and the range can be from 30 ft. upwards. One can thus be in hiding out of sight, or even in the house, and take the appropriate moment to press the release and secure the picture. True, one has to emerge and re-set the shutter afterwards, but the author's argument is that, without it, one would not have secured a photograph in any case! Shutter adapters enable this invaluable gadget to be used with most types of release.

The best place to start your bird photography is in the garden, where one can work in one's own time, in privacy, and where our subjects can be lured towards us by means of feeding devices or nest boxes. Here of course the remote control is an essential. Experience in the garden will, too, stand you in good stead when you go forth into the field complete with hide and all the other gear necessary for a wider range of subjects. Some of the best pictures the author has taken were by means of a stake pushed into the lawn, between the garden proper and the feeding devices, with the camera on a tripod, focused on the top of the stake, which appeared in the lower part of the picture. By this means robin, great tit, greenfinch, and even brambling, were photographed one winter, using the remote control from indoors. The interruption incurred in going out-of-doors to re-set the camera was momentary, and the birds soon came back to have their portraits taken – these in colour.

Bird photography can also be undertaken, without infringing any laws or rules, in most of the bird reserves belonging to national bodies. You might even be able to obtain permission to work on a private estate or large garden. But *never* put a hide up where the general public has access; it will soon be demolished or damaged!

Whether to use monochrome or colour film depends largely on your picture size. In colour, anything larger than 35 mm (the most popular miniature size) is bound to be more expensive, while for black-and-white a larger negative size is preferable, as in this case enlargements will have to be made or obtained, and a $2\frac{1}{4}$ in. square starts off with a big advantage. In colour there are two choices : negative film, which produces colour *prints* of larger size than the original frames, or reversal film, which comes processed in the form of transparencies ready for projection or for viewing. Good monochrome prints can be obtained from these, and many of the pictures in this book were obtained in this way. If you want to see your work in print, then monochrome film should be your first choice – some reliable camera like the Rolleicord or its many imitators will do this admirably. The author carries two cameras – a single-lens reflex loaded with colour, and a twin-lens reflex for black-and-white. There is ample choice in either model.

The author has deliberately refrained from discussing cine photography, partly because he has had little experience of it in the field, and partly because 'still' photography must come first of all if the would-be enthusiast is to build on a sound basis before tackling the very different field of the moving picture.

To close this chapter, the only photograph connected with this book which was taken from a hide was the little owl, which involved nearly two hours' wait for the bird to appear. It was taken with flash, as were several other pictures reproduced here. A small flash-bulb apparatus, which can be used with almost any type of camera, is preferable to the more expensive electronic gear, which can be valuable if you are *constantly* doing flash work.

Further reading:
The Art of Bird Photography: Hosking and Newberry. *Country Life,* 1944
Bird Photography as a Hobby: Hosking and Newberry. *Country Life*
The Technique of Bird Photography: John Warham. Focal Press, 1956
(These books are out-of-print but can be obtained in libraries or occasionally in second-hand bookshops.
And Eye for a Bird: Erice Hosking with Frank Lane. Hutchinson, 1970
(This is our premier bird photographer's autobiography, superbly illustrated in colour and monochrome and is full of invaluable advice and information, including the fact that he, too, started with a Box Brownie!)

CHAPTER ELEVEN

Tape recording

The past twenty years have added a new dimension to the bird watcher's range – tape-recording. How lucky to be able to record bird songs and calls, monitor them while recording (in some cases) play them back immediately, edit and even use them as background to amateur film! It is certainly not as cash- or time-consuming as may be assumed. The purpose of this chapter is to describe in completely non-technical language how to obtain acceptable recordings on medium-priced apparatus for your own interest – or even amusement – without going into the expense of hi-fi, stereo and all that. As in photography one must learn to walk first, and having got over that achievement, then we can look to new horizons where the possibilities are limitless.

Dr Ludwig Koch's pioneer work in sound-recording paved the way for all of us, although up to the end of the last war tape-recording was completely unknown to most of us. He had to use a complicated system of recording direct on to wax discs which had to be kept at a certain temperature while the recordings were being made; he could only use the now out-of-date speed of 78 r.p.m. because that was the *only* one, and it took literally a pantechnicon to house the elaborate equipment, cables, etc., used. His reminiscences are encouraging and delightful to read, especially when we consider the complete ease with which we can make today instant sound-recordings even in our own gardens.

A lot of money and effort can be spent wastefully on buying

and using unsuitable equipment. The high-pressure salesman, like the one in the camera shop, may persuade you that only such-and-such a make of battery tape recorder is of any use for bird recording, but has he ever done any, we may well ask! Practical experience in the field is the only way of assessing whether apparatus comes up to your expectations or not. Obviously the choice for recording 'in the field' has to be a battery type. Therefore its portability and simplicity are of paramount consideration. If we aim at making recordings up to BBC standards, then we have to consider buying a piece of apparatus that may cost as much as £250 – and there is always time later on! A suitable recorder need not weigh more than 8 or 9 lb. The ease of setting it up is most important, as a more complicated type can be frustrating when one finds that, having gone through the 'drill' and is ready to record, the bird is either silent or has flown!

The speed at which a tape-recorder records and plays back governs the quality of the sound we get. The B.B.C. will look at nothing less than 15 i.p.s. (inches per second) and that is the standard they use. One can obtain excellent fidelity at the next slower speed – $7\frac{1}{2}$ i.p.s., but few except expensive recorders will play at that speed in the field. The so-called standard recorder, the one which is most used by amateurs and is the more 'domestic' type, runs at $3\frac{3}{4}$ i.p.s., and here we get a very good result entirely acceptable to most human ears. The next speed down the scale is the one which has been used by the author for very many years – $1\frac{7}{8}$ i.p.s., which is incorporated in large numbers of makes of portable apparatus.

The main objective of the author's recordings was to put on tape the songs and calls that birds made so that they could be used time and time again to demonstrate to students. This they succeeded in doing, and nobody questioned their fidelity to nature. Provided such recordings are presented in a proper manner and not played haphazardly they have always been successful for the purpose. Your own tapes, provided they satisfy you – and they may often astonish your friends! – are all that you require. None of us is an Eric Hosking when it comes to photography, neither are we a Victor Lewis or a Margoschis when it comes to bird song recording, but so long as we get a great deal of pleasure, and *learn* by our efforts, who cares?

Having therefore decided on portability and simplicity, the beginner may think – ah! a cassette recorder, just the thing! But quite frankly, if you want any quality at all, then this rules out the latest and simplest form of recording. For one thing, it is at a still slower speed – $\frac{15}{16}$ i.p.s., and while suitable for speech or non-serious work, it is not likely to record our bird sounds with much fidelity, particularly in the high-frequency range, such as the grasshopper warbler and others. Until recently, too, it was not possible to 'edit' the cassette tape, and in any case the tape used is a narrower type which cannot be used on another machine. The standard tape is versatile, and can be used at any speed the recorder is capable of. Also, from the battery-powered recorder one can transcribe recordings on to a mains model, and this improves the quality besides discovering sounds which were not evident, although recorded.

The type of portable recorder used by the author, who was fortunate enough to be allowed to use it 'in the field' before it was purchased, is one which bore the label Philips (or Stella or Cossor), and although now some years old and 'out-of-date' commercially, it still gives as good recordings as ever. It is powered by six U2 batteries. Machines of this kind can often be picked up quite cheaply in second-hand shops – but if you can try it out before buying, all the better. Long after the author bought his model, portable tape-recorders were the subject of a test by the magazine *Which* and it was very gratifying to note that this particular machine was given high marks for fidelity, lack of background noise, and other points. Indeed, it was stated that the results were equal to those obtained with a machine costing £20 more!

There are, of course, other good makes available either new or second-hand, and if you have a friend who knows something about the business, then his advice will be invaluable and save you money and disappointment. But bear in mind you are looking for a machine to record bird songs and calls – it will do other things equally well, of course, but there is a special need for care in choosing something suitable. The microphones provided with most tape recorders are not entirely suitable for our specialised purpose. Ribbon and crystal types are little use; the one most often recommended is the *cardioid*, which has a special capability of picking up what the other types cannot. The more expensive types of microphone, such as the moving-coil, are wasted for our purpose. Quite often a microphone of the type recommended can be picked up cheaply, and it will certainly improve the quality when used instead of the one supplied with the portable set. One is provided with the sets mentioned.

The next item is a parabolic reflector, which channels the sound on to a 'dished' metal disc, the microphone being placed facing *inwards* towards the centre of the parabole. This is intended to cut out a lot of extraneous noise and to focus the sound centrally. But there is today a divergence of opinion as to the utility of this accessory. Victor Lewis, who has made many commercial disc recordings for the large record companies, has discarded the reflector and uses the 'bare' microphone everywhere. Mr Margoschis, on the other hand, who is tape editor to the Wildlife Tape Recording Society, uses the reflector invariably. So, the choice is yours. Try both ways, and you may find, like the author, that it seems to make little difference! But perhaps we have not the ultra-critical hearing of the experts! If you want to experiment with a simple reflector (and a 'commercial' one will cost you at least £10) try a metal dust-bin lid, which can be just as effective.

One thing to be guarded against is the extraneous noise evident when using such a piece of apparatus. The slightest rubbing of the cable, the touch of a hand on the perimeter, the knocking of the reflector against some object – any of these can mar an otherwise good recording. If you want to eliminate the exaggerated sound of wind in the microphone, then stretch a piece of silk or nylon stocking over the whole front of the reflector, stick it down securely, and you should have no serious trouble. You can, too, fix your reflector by means of a ball-and-socket head to the camera tripod, when it can be used to give directional recording. You can, if inclined, make your own fibre-glass reflector by following the instructions given in the work mentioned at the end of this chapter.

Now a word about tapes and tracks. You will, in tape-makers' lists, see tapes described as standard, double play, triple play and so on. This refers to the thickness of the *base* on which the magnetic material is fused; this is .002 in. thick in the standard; .001 in. in double play; and .00075 in. for triple play. These have a bearing on the amount of tape a reel contains, but the thinner tape is apt at times to imprint its recordings on to the next layer, and thus is not suitable for our purpose. Standard or long play should therefore be our choice. Again, one can get machines that play two- three- or four-tracks, i.e. : all on the same standard type of tape, which means that more than one recording can be made – up to four in fact – on the same tape, thereby effecting an enormous economy in tape use.

But so far as the recording of bird song is concerned, and indeed any other form of recording where *editing* is necessary, if one tries to do this with a tape containing more than one recorded track, then the other tracks are useless or wasted, as cutting will destroy their value. The author *never* uses any other than a single track; after all, tape is not so expensive as film, it can be used over and over again if recordings are not satisfactory. One tape of which the author is particularly proud, contains no less than forty different species of local bird made by splicing the various strips of recorded tape together, (and involving forty splices!) which makes a most attractive tape to describe the country's birds.

One of the drawbacks of the less costly tape-recorders is that they have not, like many of the mains models, a 'metering' or counting device which tells us exactly where a certain recording lies (provided always you start at 'zero' with the particular tape you wish to play!) but this is not a serious drawback and with a little practice one can get to the approximate position wanted. There is, however, a device (either a needle-type or electronic eye) which enables one to see whether one is over- or under-recording at the time.

Mention must also be made of the sizes of tape reels for use in the field. The makes previously mentioned take a 3 in. spool, or a 4 in. with the protective cover removed. The former, at 'long play', will give us half-an-hour's recording, using of course only one track. It is surprising how long it will take you to fill up this length of tape, but you can always erase effectively anything that is not satisfactory, and start again. Therefore the recorder can be run very economically indeed.

So, having equipped ourselves with what we hope will be a satisfactory piece of apparatus, and armed with tape and microphone, where better to start than in the garden, or even the local park if we do not mind carrying around something that might arouse the curiosity of the passer-by. In the garden we can try out the sparrows – it is surprising how many different calls they have when you have taped a few of them! – a robin, blackbird and so on, depending on the time of year, of course. But these first, maybe faltering, steps need not be unsuccessful. See that your 'mike' is properly adjusted in the reflector, or that you are holding the former directly at the subject; notice whether there is any reflex action from the needle or magic-eye. It may be necessary to get closer, if you can, and this is where the garden birds score over the wilder ones of the open countryside. They are usually used to you, and may not shy away from the recordist. The author has, as an experiment, recorded a blackbird in full song and then played it back immediately, greatly to the bewilderment of the singer! Anyhow, with further guidance and experience you should now be well on the way to successful tape-recording.

Mention has been made of 'splicing'. This is done with a simple piece of apparatus which comes with a razor-blade and full instructions. There is no difficulty in making perfect splices, and nothing will be heard of them on your recorder.

You can, if you wish, speak into the microphone and introduce the birds as you get them, but the author prefers to let the birds speak for themselves.

The possibilities of wild life tape recording are limitless, the rewards considerable. If you are at all keen on making progress, there is the Wildlife Sound Recording Society, Mancetter, Atherstone, Warwickshire, which will welcome your membership, issues bulletins and organises tape-recording courses, besides running competitions which are broadcast by the BBC in the 'Living World' programmes. There is probably today more scope in tape-recording than in photography for the wild life enthusiast, and future developments hold out great possibilities of video-tape, stereo and other almost unexplored fields, where patience and originality are the main assets.

Further reading:
Bird Song Recording: F. Purves. Focal Press, 1962
Memoirs of a Birdman: Ludwig Koch. Phoenix House, 1955
Natural History Sound Recording: R. Margoschis. Print & Press Service Ltd, 1970
(This is Part I of an encyclopaedia of tape recording, but can be purchased separately.)

CHAPTER TWELVE

Sketching birds

The author has long been convinced that drawing should be very much easier than writing. The caveman, with bits of charcoal derived from his wood fires, and ochres and clays from the surrounding earth, drew on his exceedingly rough walls lifelike pictures of wild creatures *in action* – vital lines and poses that few could emulate today after a course of cubes and prisms, plaster casts and the other dead clutter of the 'art class'. Yet he had no lessons in drawing from life, no art teachers; he could not *write* as we know it, for he had neither language nor grammar.

Writing is a difficult subject for the child. It has to be taught certain hieroglyphics that have to be converted by hand and ear into sounds – ay, bee, cee, dee and so on. These peculiar marks on paper have then to be written *and* spoken. Yet if you give a child a piece of paper and a pencil, as soon as he or she is capable of holding the latter it will immediately begin to use it, although only making mere scribbles on paper. But, *without being taught,* in a short time the child will produce a house or a bird; crude enough, it is true, but recognisable! And this is years before it is able to even put down those hieroglyphics with confidence. Thus the eye, through the mind, controls the hand so that the object is drawn without any training or confusion.

There is nothing so satisfying as an outdoor sketch-book, whether your subject be trees, lych gates, old houses or birds. You don't *have* to be an 'artist' to put down the essentials. But, the objection invariably arises, 'I can't draw a straight line!' You don't have to! Get yourself a *ring-bound* sketch-book about 7 in. x 5 in. with cartridge paper. This type opens flat, which is necessary for outdoor work. A BB *carbon* pencil and a soft indiarubber complete the outfit. Later on, when some progress has been made, you can tackle a larger size, but you will inevitably waste some pages at first, so the smaller the book the less will be the wastage.

Now just consider for a few moments the basic fact that every bird came from an egg and the shape of an egg is retained during the whole of its life, whether the bird is viewed in profile, head-on, flying or just sitting. It does not matter what type of bird you consider – owl, woodpecker, duck, robin, puffin – they all have that basic shape to begin with. Go back to Chapter Five, Recognition, and you will recollect that a large number of species can be recognised by shape and size alone, without bothering about markings, colour or sound. When a child draws its first bird it is more often than not a crude representation, but it has contrived to get down on paper something remarkably like that creature which evolved, millions and millions of years ago, from the sea – the head is cod-like, the rudimentary wings were derived from fins, the scales become feathers and the rudder a tail. Go out into the garden or park and just look at the birds you can find – could you do better than the child? But once we keep in mind that basic shape – the egg – there is no reason why we should not, after some practice, begin to put down something that resembles a bird.

Look at the stage-by-stage sketches in this chapter. The wings are not 'stuck on' as the child's are; the head is supported by a neck; the legs, too, are not like match-sticks but develop naturally from the body. (Incidentally, the bird's knee as such is within the body; what we see outside, facing the tail, is the bird's ankle, so that for the most part birds are literally walking on their toes.)

Your first efforts may disappoint, but if you persevere and keep doing these preliminary sketches, (even indoors if you

The *basic facts* – draw the egg first and build your bird around it. After some experience you will learn to sketch without first drawing the egg

prefer), they will become slicker and more lively as you progress. Don't press on the paper, keep your wrist free; only the little finger should be used to glide over the paper. But this won't come all at once. Don't sharpen your pencil to a fine point;

make it wedge-shaped so that you can use thick and thin lines as necessary.

After filling some pages you may be encouraged to sketch parts of a bird – a wing or tail, head and beak, and so on. Young birds in particular are fairly easy to draw: a round

Some sketch-book notes of birds in action. Never mind if you cannot at first get down the whole bird. Stick to the essential lines. And always remember the egg-shape whether the bird is sitting, flying, swimming or just perching

shape with downy outline, a large eye, and a typical 'nestling beak' – quite easy! Before you go into the field with your sketch-book, try to envisage what you are going to do – not to put down every feather, but to get the basic *shape*, the difference between say a sparrow and a pigeon, or the head of a rook and that of an owl. These little exercises will familiarise you with the differences between various birds and help you in recognition. Sketches of a bird showing, say, distinctive wing patches, or tail pattern, are invaluable. They have in the past enabled the author, together with suitable notes based on the code described in our preface, to obtain confirmation of unusual birds, the sketches being undisputed proof of identities.

The one big objection to sketching birds is that they move! They don't keep still! But don't let that discourage you. If you can get down a few basic lines to start with – and you may fill pages and pages with them – you will be making steady progress. You will eventually realise that sketching a bird can be fun and can help enormously with identification problems. So keep at it all the year round.

To make detailed drawings or paintings of birds is quite another matter. Here you must either be absolutely familiar with the bird you are portraying, or refer to coloured plates where detailed figures are available, but that is another art from that of sketching. You can, if you are within reasonable reach of a museum, sketch your birds from the many mounted specimens you will find there – and learn a lot about the shape and size and plumage of the bird in addition – but that, while by no means time-wasting, cannot be compared with sketching in the field. A couple of hours with the ducks in a park or the inhabitants of a zoo, will again give you much practice and confidence, but your field work is the most important, and the most rewarding. Many people cannot go out into the country and sketch or paint where there are onlookers; a deserted stretch of canal, a lonely moorland, an unfrequented woodland track, a secluded valley, even an old orchard, should give you 'sitters' at any time of year, and as previously mentioned, there

Some more sketch-book notes. Note how the eye of the bird gives *life* to the drawing; don't make a black blob – the eye has a 'catch light' in it which makes all the difference between life and dullness. (All these sketch-book notes were originally drawn twice their present size)

is a lot of scope in your own garden, even from the comfort of the house.

This chapter is necessarily brief; it aims to give you the *basic* principles, and if you are sincerely interested, a list of excellent books on the subject follows. These are written by professional artists who understand their birds, and they will teach you much more than the rudiments of a fascinating branch of bird study. Your library may have one or two of them in stock; if not, they can be obtained through other branches, or, again, from second-hand bookshops. All of them are very well worthwhile. So, good sketching, and success to your efforts.

Further reading:
Bird Portraiture: C. F. Tunnicliffe, RA. Studio Publications, 1945
How I draw Birds: Roland Green. A. & C. Black, 1951
How to Draw Birds: Raymond Sheppard. Studio Publications, 1940
More Birds to Draw: Raymond Sheppard. Studio Publications, 1956
Wing Tips: Roland Green. A. & C. Black, 1947

CHAPTER THIRTEEN

Practical bird study

Apart from enjoying our avian population by simply watching and enjoying the vitality of birds, there are numerous ways in which we can not only usefully increase our own knowledge but add to the sum of man's still incomplete appreciation of the many unsolved problems of the bird world and its relationship with man. Mention has already been made of enquiries into the status and changes in population and distribution of birds, of censuses and special investigations carried out by such bodies as the British Trust for Ornithology. Migration has already been cited as a fascinating but by no means completely understood feature of bird life. The lives of many of our commonest species have by no means been worked out completely, and the amateur often provides valuable information and facts for the ornithologist.

Take the starling, for instance, one of our commonest and most familiar birds, which even a city dweller might with advantage take up as a special study, without neglecting other species or everyday bird watching. Have you ever seen, or been in, a starling roost? Vast winter roosts occur almost everywhere except in hilly regions, and even in our cities, numbering from a few thousand to at times over a million birds. Studies have been made of them by keen amateurs, but there is still much to be discovered. These roosts usually last about a couple of months, then, almost suddenly, the place is deserted as though by mutual consent, and the nightly rendezvous occurs elsewhere, perhaps miles away. A regular watcher discovered that rats patrol these roosts nightly, picking up dead birds that inevitably occur in such vast gatherings. The all-night clamour of a starling roost has to be experienced to be believed, and the astonishing aerial evolutions that precede roosting, around dusk, are one of the sights that never fail to thrill every bird watcher. Here, too, is a great opportunity not only for bird photography with flash and high-speed film, but for some interesting tape-recording! And what about the morning departure patterns?

Starlings are by no means the only birds that form communal roosts. Swallows and Martins, ready for 'off' in late autumn, gather in thousands in suitable reed beds (as also do starlings), safe from predators. Redwings, too, often congregate in trees and sing in chorus before leaving us for their Scandinavian homes in March and April. Bramblings, also winter visitors, often make up large roosts in wooded areas; gulls of all species except the kittiwake, which is usually only a summer visitor to Britain, congregate in tens of thousands on lakes and meres.

Where do our commonest birds – thrush, blackbird, robin and others – roost? We know that wrens will often use our garden nest-boxes for mutual warmth; indeed, after the hard winter of 1962–63 the pathetic skeletons and feathers of *twenty-four* wrens were found in *one* box! Pied wagtails are known to roost in the roofs of noisy factories, probably for warmth and mutual protection, and there is a well-known roost of this species, sometimes numbering two thousand, in the centre of Dublin! The scope is wide, and ringing groups would be glad of news and help in this respect.

Even in your garden or local park there is scope for the study of bird behaviour, changes in population and species, breeding successes and many other aspects.

There is still another aspect of bird life in which the amateur can help considerably – the economics of ornithology. What do our birds eat and how does it affect our own lives? Are there 'harmful' and 'beneficial' birds? How is food related to environment and agriculture? Many years ago Walter Collinge, a scientist and lecturer, published a most important work *The Food of Some British Wild Birds* (Dulau & Co, 1913). It contained the results of many years' study and research, both in the field and the laboratory, and dealt with some thirty common species, totalling over 3,000 adults and some 300 nestlings. This unique work would not be possible today, as the victims were shot, trapped, or otherwise obtained, and the contents of stomach, crop and pellet scientifically examined so thoroughly that the exact species of creature (field vole, common shrew, mole, grasshopper, beetle, etc.) was identified, and so too was the vegetable matter – seed husks, grain, berries, fruits, etc., not only in the breeding season but all the year round and in various parts of the country. Thus a vast amount of information was tabulated, proving beyond doubt the feeding habits of the birds concerned. Although this work was subsequently re-published, it has long been out-of-print and still forms the only reference work of its kind.

Many detailed papers on the subject of the food of wild birds have appeared in scientific journals and the transactions of ornithological societies, but there is still much more to be done. Changes in bird population and distribution, the arrival of such birds as the collared dove, the vast revolutions in agriculture and forestry that have taken place since Collinge's day, together with the new world of insecticides, pesticides, herbicides and fertilizers, have changed the whole character of research and economics, and again the amateur can help.

One of the most interesting aspects of research into the food of wild birds is the collection and dissection of pellets, thrown up not only by all the owls and birds of prey, but by rooks and crows, heron, kingfisher, and even our garden robin. These pellets consist of the *undigested* matter – bones, fur, feathers, skulls, wing cases, etc., periodically disgorged through the beak. Their examination will reveal, even to the beginner, the obvious food of the owls, for instance – the remains of mice, voles, rats, small birds, etc. These birds, and herons and kingfishers, bolt their prey whole, head first, and the rejected remains form pellets later thrown up. In this way, over a period, it has been proved without shadow of doubt, for instance, that a pair of barn owls will, in a year, account for some two thousand mice, voles and young rats! As many as four skulls of such creatures can often be found in a single pellet.

Owls throw up pellets either near their nesting holes or in a nearby roosting spot – often an old, hollow oak tree, and here, if they are regularly collected, they can be easily dissected in a dish of warm water. The solid remains can be mounted on cards and possibly identified correctly by a biologist friend, but in any case the type of prey taken is obvious. Quite a few schools up and down the country do this kind of thing, which is to be encouraged, as it not only helps to reveal the economic importance of owls and other birds, but leads to an appreciation of wild bird life by the schools.

At the same time, useful collections of bird feathers can be made without harm to the species. Birds picked up dead or that have been killed on roads, feathers from moulting places in autumn, such as those by the watersides used by ducks and geese; a gamekeeper's gibbet will usually yield feathers of magpie, jay and maybe an unfortunate and wrongly-accused owl will be obtained, perhaps even a kestrel or sparrow hawk. It is useful to be able to recognise the exact part of a bird from which the feathers are obtained.

Nest watching, without disturbing the birds, can often be profitable. How many times in, say, a couple of hours, do the parents visit the nest with food? In the case of owls, particularly the tawny, it is advisable to be well under cover, or wear goggles or fencing mask, as this bird is, naturally, most aggressive when feeding young, and will unhesitatingly attack any suspicious creature lurking in the vicinity of the nest. It will just as surely attack a human being or a dog passing beneath the site, whether the passer-by is aware of the nest or not!

There is, however, a less hazardous occupation! Watch a nest box or nest hole when the parent is feeding the brood. In only half-an-hour's vigil you will find that blue tits visit the nest every four or five minutes, each time with a beakful of small green caterpillars as a rule – remember these broods are 'timed' to coincide with the hatch of millions of caterpillars! – and if you work this out in a dawn-to-dusk day you will be impressed by the amount of food consumed by the hungry and growing nestlings. Even the house sparrow, a seed-eater by its hard beak, has a breeding season of some three months, and feeds it young entirely on grubs, caterpillars, maggots, insects and other animal matter, as do all small birds for that matter. There is certainly plenty of scope for the amateur!

Another sphere where the amateur who is scientifically inclined may be interested is the study of avian parasitology. Birds, like other living creatures including man, have a number of natural parasites that mostly live in 'harmony' with their host. Known as commensalism, this is where one of the partners benefits, usually the parasite, but no harm is usually caused to the host. Blood suckers, feather lice, ticks, bugs, intestinal worms, flukes and many other creatures batten on the living bird.

Mention has already been made of the parasites left in nest boxes. The Swift, which does not come to land except accidentally or to creep into its nest crevice, is unable to bathe either in dust or water, and must therefore carry its quota of parasites for life! Our Cuckoo is of course parasitic on other species. At many ringing stations these parasites are removed for analysis and classification, and many valuable lessons can be learnt from their study. It may sound 'creepy-crawly' but there are many people studying the subject, which has some bearing on human life.

There is an eminently readable yet thoroughly knowledgeable book on the subject – *Fleas, Flukes and Cuckoos*, by Miriam Rothschild and Theresa Clay, published in the New Naturalist Library (Collins) in 1957 and in Arrow Books' paper back in 1961. It is still obtainable and is well worth reading if only for the astonishing facts it contains, For instance, when the sand martin goes back to Africa in the autumn, it leaves its parasites in the nest-hole. When the time comes for the birds to return to their breeding habitat, the parasites are waiting at the edge of the nest-holes to greet them!

Many monographs on individual species of bird have been published from time to time, from the days of Edgar Chance's remarkable books on our native cuckoo. Not many years ago the author was assured by an old countryman that the cuckoo goes into a hollow tree in the autumn, moults and turns into a sparrow hawk! (Note the similarity in plumage and *shape* between these two birds, and you will understand why small birds mob it – not because of its reprehensible habits but because it *looks* like a hawk!) When the cuckoo's egg is laid in the foster-parent's nest the latter treat it as one of their own in spite of its somewhat different size and often markings. When the youngster hatches (which it does more quickly than the rightful chicks because its egg has a thinner shell) it begins to throw out any other eggs or young that are in the nest, and the foster-parents take not the slightest notice of these unfortunate progeny of their own; what concerns them is what is *inside* the rim of the nest! How do young cuckoos, which leave us some time after the adult cuckoos have left our shores, find their way, unaided, to West Africa? There is enough material in this one species for very many more original studies!

To conclude, a lot of nonsense is often heard about parent birds 'teaching' their fledgelings to fly, to sing, or to make nests. They do none of these things. Nestlings reared away from sight and sound of their parents instinctively sing, fly and build nests without any instruction. They have inborn senses which humans have never possessed. Truly the world of birds is full of endless mystery and fascination. If bird watching is for you, then you have a lifetime of interest and exploration in front of you. Nobody is either too young or too old to begin a study in which this book has but touched the fringe.

Birds and the law

The laws regarding wild birds are by no means as simple as may be supposed although, with certain exceptions, *all* wild birds, their nests and eggs are now protected in the breeding season. The Protection of Birds Act 1954 repealed no less than fifteen previous Acts, and, with the Protection of Birds Act 1967, forms the basis of our present legislation on the subject. It has been truly said, however, that every Act of Parliament has its loopholes and none is perfect. The clever law-breaker can find his way through the legal jargon and phraseology. Nevertheless our British wild birds now have a 'deal' which is second to none. Basically, the principal Act (1954) lays down that any person who wilfully

kills, injures or takes *any wild bird* or
takes, damages or destroys the nest of any wild
bird while that nest is in use or
Takes or destroys the egg of any wild bird

is guilty of an offence against the Act.

This means, broadly, that egg-collecting, even by schoolboys, is quite illegal and that the trapping of wild birds, except under licence for ringing purposes, is also an offence. It is also illegal to sell British birds' eggs, to offer them for sale or even to exchange them. The maximum penalty in regard to a 'common' bird is £5 for each egg, nest, skin or bird; for birds in the First Schedule of the Act it is £25, or a term of imprisonment, or both!

Appendix I Birds and the law

The First Schedule includes the following species, protected *at all times*:

Avocet
Bittern
Buzzard, Honey
Chough
Corncrake
Crossbill
Curlew, Stone
Diver (all species)
Dotterel
Eagle (all species)
Goshawk
Grebe, Black-necked
Grebe, Slavonian
Greenshank
Harriers (all species)
Hobby
Hoopoe
Kite
Merlin
Oriole, Golden
Osprey

Owl, Barn
Peregrine Falcon
Phalarope, Red-necked
Plover, Little Ringed
Quail
Redstart, Black
Ruff and Reeve
Shrike, Red-backed
Sparrow Hawk
Spoonbill
Stint, Temminck's
Swan, Bewick's
Swan, Whooper
Tern, Black
Tern, Roseate
Tit, Bearded
Tit, Crested
Warbler, Dartford
Warbler, Marsh
Wren, St Kilda
Wryneck

The following birds and their eggs are protected by special penalties *during the close season:*

Brambling
Duck, Long-tailed
Garganey
Godwit, Black-tailed
Golden-eye

Goose, Greylag
Scaup
Scoter, Common
Scoter, Velvet
Whimbrel

There are others, even rarer, and the list contains those birds which, by nesting rarely or irregularly in Britain, or are seriously declining in numbers, need this special protection.

The Second Schedule lists birds 'which *may* be killed or taken at any time *by authorised persons*'.

Cormorant	Jay
Crow, Carrion and Hooded	Magpie
Dove, Collared (Scotland only)	Merganser (Scotland only)
Dove, Rock (Scotland only)	Pigeon (domestic gone feral)*
Dove, Stock	Pigeon, Wood
Goosander (Scotland only)	Rook
Gull, Greater Black-backed	Shag
Gull Herring	Sparrow, House
Gull Lesser Black-backed	Starling
Jackdaw	

The 'authorised person' can be an owner or occupier of land, or any person authorised by him, i.e. a gamekeeper or farmer, who could say that any of these birds were causing damage among gamebirds or to food crops.

There are two more schedules to the Act. The Third Schedule concerns birds which may be taken or killed outside the close season, consisting of such game birds as duck, curlew, plover, snipe, etc., and geese. The Fourth Schedule is of birds which may *not* be sold alive unless close-ringed and bred in captivity, and lists most of our smaller birds, particularly those which used to be popular cage birds or which could breed in captivity. The term 'close-ringed' means that the ring must have been affixed to the nestling and *not* to an adult, thus assuming the bird to be 'aviary-bred'. There is, however, a loophole here : bird trappers have been known to find nests of these birds in the wild, and to ring the chicks just before they are ready to 'fledge' or leave the nest, and then take them into an aviary; it would be hard to prove that the birds were not reared in captivity!

It is illegal to take wild birds by means of traps, snares, bird lime and the use of live decoys. This is still prevalent in many parts of the country, hence the numerous prosecutions initiated

*feral=wild.

by the R.S.P.B., the R.S.P.C.A. and the police. It is also illegal to set up pole traps (they have been outlawed for many years but are still used) even on private land, and the R.S.P.B. is currently conducting a nationwide campaign against this cruel method.

The practice of taking young birds of prey for training in so-called falconry is entirely illegal. Even the experienced falconer has to apply to the Home Office for a permit to possess and use a falcon, and in present circumstances a British-taken bird would not be sanctioned.

It is even illegal to use either mist or rocket nets to catch wild birds, but the qualified ringer can obtain a licence to use such traps and to ring or mark the birds so caught, but they have to be released without delay. A police constable may stop and search any vehicle, without a warrant, if he suspects any contravention of the Acts, and may also arrest a person if that person fails to give his name and address. (It is not unusual for egg-collecting equipment – drills, blow-pipes, and cotton-wool-lined boxes – to be found in the vehicles of suspects).

Nothing has yet been said about illegal shooting. There is quite a lot of this still going on, particularly in estuaries where wild geese and duck abound in winter. 'Marsh cowboys' is the term used for the gentry that practise it, and birds are often left to die miserably when they cannot be reached easily. It is illegal for anyone under fourteen to own an air or shot gun, and it must not be used by anyone within 50 ft. of a public highway, road or footpath; neither must it be carried loaded. If you see any obviously breaking the law, try to contact the local police, the R.S.P.C.A. or the local bird society, by telephone if possible and give full details. If a vehicle is involved, take its registration number. You are also entitled to ask if the person has permission to shoot on the land.

If you witness, or suspect, birds being trapped (other than by authorised ringers of course) either on waste land, commons, or even in gardens, again contact an authority quickly; the great thing is to have such offenders 'caught in the act'.

There are many other things mentioned in the Acts, much too technical to merit mention here, but the above is a basic outline of the main principles and objects. Much of the above has been condensed from the literature available from the R.S.P.B., The Lodge, Sandy, Bedfordshire, and the interested reader is recommended to write for the free publications listed below, enclosing, of course, a stamp with your application :

Air Gun Users Beware!: a leaflet setting out the Law in plain language, and what to do.

Bird Photography and The Law: a leaflet dealing with the birds in Schedule 1 of the 1954 Act, and where to apply for approval.

Information on Feeding Birds: a folder giving useful advice as to bird tables, food, etc., and a list of shrubs attractive to birds.

The Safe use of Pesticides in the Garden: what not to use, and the safe ones.

Treatment of Sick and Injured Birds: a valuable booklet which may save many lives and shows the right and wrong ways of dealing with bird casualties.

Wild Birds and the Law: a fully descriptive pamphlet which deals more fully with the Acts and their purposes.

Bibliography

The books selected by the author are a small part of his collection. Only those which he has read and found useful either in the field or for further study have been included. The reader is urged to seek out in public libraries and bookshops, both new and second-hand, all the bird books that are available. As with every other subject there are good books and indifferent ones. Competent reviews of ornithological literature appear often in the periodicals devoted to the subject – *Ibis, British Birds, Bird Study, Birds,* and also in *The Countryman, Country Life, The Field, Countryside* and many others, all written by experienced and qualified people.

Older books, especially those of the ninteenth and early twenteenth centuries, are often attractive and indeed valuable, but obviously the information as to distribution and status of birds is now out-of-date and could give the beginner a misleading picture and a false impression. For instance, one of the best all-round popular bird books, first published in the 1880s was Rev C. A. John's *British Birds in their Haunts* (he also wrote companion volumes on wild flowers and trees), which was originally illustrated with woodcuts, but in 1909 a handsome volume appeared, illustrated with coloured figures by an unknown artist, W. Foster. These figures have scarcely been bettered in any other work, and a few years ago a reprint appeared on the market with the original plates but with the text revised. The older editions, however, omit such birds as the willow tit (not then differentiated from the marsh tit), the little owl and the Canada goose. So there is much to be said for the up-to-date guide, of which several are available today. Indeed, the bird watcher is presented with a bewildering array of attractive books, covering all aspects of bird study.

REFERENCE BOOKS

Birds of the British Isles & *Their Eggs:* T. A. Coward.

This standard work has now become a classic and has been re-issued several times. It is in three comparatively small volumes, has colour plates by Thorburn, one of our best artists. A very valuable guide for the beginner. Published by Fredk. Warne & Co.

British Birds: Kirkman & Jourdain.

First published 1935, reprinted since, with 200 coloured plates by well-known bird artists, depicting birds in their natural surroundings. This is a large volume quite recently re-issued at £2, and is a handsome book, also containing plates of all British birds' eggs, which is unusual today in any book. The text deals in factual form with descriptions, habitat, food, usual notes, etc. Published by T. Nelson & Sons.

The Handbook of British Birds: Witherby, Jourdain, Ticehurst & Tucker.

First published March 1938; reprinted and revised since; five volumes.

This is popularly known as the 'bird watcher's bible' and contains every known fact about British birds up to the date of publication, plus coloured plates of all the species on the British list at that time, and showing in most cases adult male and female, juveniles, etc. Many distribution maps and full detailed descriptions of plumage, measurements, etc. Song tables and other useful information is also given.

This work fetches anything from £15 to £20 second-hand, and has, ever since first publication, been regarded as the standard work. Published by H. F. & G. Witherby, London.

The Popular Handbook of British Birds: P. A. D. Hollom.

This is a single volume based on *The Handbook*. It lays special emphasis on field identification and is thoroughly up-to-date. There are 136 colour plates and, with the exception of extremely rare vagrants, is comprehensive. Published by H. F. & G. Witherby.

FIELD GUIDES

Field Guide to the Birds of Britain & Europe: Peterson, Mountfort & Hollom.

First issued 1954. This has also gone into several editions, and contains practically all the European birds. It would probably dismay the beginner as there are so many species not known in Britain, but for the intending European traveller it is excellent. The birds are in the scientific order, the descriptions are brief but well condensed; there are distribution maps for most species, a check list and excellent chapters on identification, topography, and recognition of special features, etc. The coloured figures are by Roger Peterson, America's greatest living bird artist. Published by Collins.

The Hamlyn Guide to Birds of Britain & Europe: B. Bruun & A. Singer.

First issued 1970. This is the third of the comprehensive 'field guides' – there are others to follow! It is really a paperback in a fairly stout cover; the plates and descriptions again cover all the European species, with the big advantage that descriptions and distribution maps face the coloured figures – a very valuable time-saving feature. The figures are excellent, there are plenty of 'flight' as well as 'perched' figures. Here again the beginner may get confused. These guides are really for those who have had some experience in the field; nevertheless they are most attractive and should eventually become a 'must'. Published by Hamlyn.

How to Know British Birds: Norman Joy.

First issued 1936, fourth impression 1942. I have put in this little book because it should be quite easy to pick it up at a jumble sale or in a second-hand bookshop for a small sum, yet it has afforded the author most valuable information in regard to field characteristics, voice and song. The coloured and other plates are not outstanding but are to be regarded as 'guides' only; the text is highly condensed, the book is pocketable and there are good classified notes on song, environment, etc. It could well be revised and re-issued. Published by H. F. and G. Witherby.

Pocket Guide to British Birds: R. S. R. Fitter & R. A. Richardson.

First issued 1952 and re-issued several times since, this is possibly the first real field guide, presenting the birds in a novel way, by size and habitat. The plates, too, are original in grouping together birds which have similar appearance or markings. On most plates is the silhouette of a sparrow in exact scale with the birds shown. The text begins at the smallest species (Goldcrest) and works up to the swans. There are excellent chapters on plumage, migration, songs and calls, etc. The preliminary chapters are essential reading. Published by Collins, London.

GUIDE TO BIRD WATCHING

Bird Watching for Beginners: Dr Bruce Campbell and R. A. Richardson.

This is written in a less scientific way than the last named, and is by one of our foremost ornithologists. It describes the British birds in their classifications, with maps and useful line drawings; problems of bird watching such as counts and surveys, migration, behaviour and photography. Penguin Books, 1952.

Collins' Guide to Bird Watching: Fitter.

This is an excellent and practical book, published in 1963,

showing how to watch birds, what to watch for, where to look, and a very detailed topographical guide to the whole of the British Isles, giving county by county the habitats, special birds, reserves, societies, local literature, etc. It is illustrated with first-class photographs of both birds and their habitats. It is not an identification guide, but the birds of each type of habitat are well described. Published by Collins.

Watching Birds: James Fisher.

First published 1941. Reprinted 1946. This was one of the early Penguin series, written by an outstanding ornithologist and writer. It aims to introduce the bird watcher to the birds by chapters on scientific arrangement, migration, territory, courtship and many other aspects of bird life. The illustrations are all line drawings from the wings of a pterodactyl and bat, to maps of reed bunting territories near Oxford. Well worth reading. Published by Penguin Books.

There are very many other bird books well worthy of perusal but they are too numerous to describe here. The A.A. *Book of British Birds*, for instance, is not a *field* guide, and although the colour illustrations are excellent, many of them appear to have been taken from museum specimens, as the ducks and geese are all standing on the water's edge, which they seldom do when the bird watcher approaches! Nevertheless, it is a good book, and the little pocket recognition guide sold with it is quite useful.

BOOKS FOR THE LIBRARY :

Birds as Individuals: Len Howard. Collins, 1952.
Bird Ringing: Lockley & Russell. Lockwood, 1953.
British Birds in Their Haunts: Rev C. A. Johns. Revised, 1909 and reprinted since. Routledge.
The Charm of Birds: Earl Grey of Fallodon, Hodder, 1927 and reprinted since.

Down the Long Wind: Garth Christian. Newnes, 1961.
Enjoying Ornithology: Dr David Lack, Methuen, 1965.
How to Study Birds: Stuart Smith. Collins, 1945.
Natural History of Selborne: Gilbert White. The first book describing birds 'in the field' directly. Scores of editions to date.
The Shell Bird Book: James Fisher. Ebury Press, 1966.
Territory in Bird Life: Eliot Howard. Collins, 1948.

In addition to the above, there are many excellent books by bird photographers and bird artists; monographs on such species as the wood pigeon, yellow wagtail, redstart, hawfinch – even the house sparrow – and the older pioneer books by Oliver Pike and the Kearton brothers, describing early difficulties and triumphs at the turn of the century. Many booksellers specialise in ornithology, and their lists are certainly worth perusing. New books are constantly appearing, describing expeditions to places that a generation ago would have seemed unlikely or even unthinkable, but the whole world of birds is still being explored and described by camera and pen.

Ornithological organisations

A number of national bodies are concerned with bird life; the principal ones are listed below. In addition, there are such bodies as the Nature Conservancy (part of the Natural Environment Research Council), which owns certain reserves and has powers to declare sites of special scientific interest if the status and situation warrants it; The National Trust, a private body which owns certain nature reserves such as the Farne Islands, Scolt Head (Norfolk) and others; The Council for Nature, Zoological Gardens, London N.W.1, the national body representing the voluntary natural history and conservation movement. These cover any branch of wild life interest if the need arises.

There are in most counties bird clubs, ornithological societies, amateur naturalist organisations and field clubs, all doing good work in their own localities, and which welcome new members. Details can always be obtained about their activities, subscriptions, etc., from local libraries.

The following organisations may be described as the 'official' ones for all classes of bird watcher from the professional to the beginner :

British Naturalists' Association, Willowfield, Boyneswood Road, Four Marks, Alton, Hampshire.

Founded 1905 to study all branches of natural history. Has many branches all over the country which hold outings and lectures. The association holds an annual field week. Publishes

Countryside, thrice yearly. Membership open to all interested in wildlife.

British Ornithologists' Union, c/o The Bird Room, The Natural History Museum, London S.W.7.

The senior scientific body in this country, dealing mainly with matters that concern the expert, and ranging over the whole field of the subject. Membership is subject to nomination by existing members. Also runs the British Ornithological Club, and publishes *Ibis* a scientific quarterly.

British Trust for Ornithology, Beech Grove, Tring, Hertfordshire.

Controls the national bird-ringing scheme; conducts enquiries into status of birds; currently engaged in producing an atlas of British breeding birds. Publishes *Bird Study* quarterly, *BTO News,* a bulletin for bird watchers, and various pamphlets. Membership open to all.

Field Studies Council, 9 Devereux Court, Strand, London W.C.2.

Has nine residential centres where amateurs of all ages may partake in outdoor activities including the study of bird life. Publishes *Field Study.*

Royal Society for the Protection of Birds, The Lodge, Sandy, Bedfordshire.

Founded in 1889, has over thirty bird reserves in Britain (to which members are admitted free by permit); conducts prosecutions against bird-trappers, egg-collectors, and campaigns to end oil pollution and other menaces such as illegal pole traps, etc. Organises film shows in all parts of the country and produces many booklets and pamphlets. Publishes *Birds* a bimonthly magazine dealing with all aspects of preservation and conservation. Membership open.

The Wildfowl Trust, Slimbridge, Gloucestershire.

Formed in 1946 to further the study of wildfowl – ducks, geese and swans; has a collection of the world's wildfowl at its headquarters; there are now other branches. Membership open. Publishes various pamphlets and reports.

Appendix III Ornithological organisations

Young Ornithologists' Club, address as for R.S.P.B.
The junior organisation which runs courses, outings and other activities. Publishes *Bird Life* a quarterly for members. Membership open to all young people.

The following publications are issued independently of any of the above :

Birds & Country Magazine: 79 Surbiton Hill Park, Surbiton, Surrey.
A quarterly illustrated magazine both for newcomers and the more experience bird watcher. Deals with other aspects of wild life as well.
British Birds: Macmillan Journals Ltd., Brunel Road, Basingstoke, Hampshire.
An old-established monthly magazine dealing with all aspects of bird life; book reviews, news, letters, etc. Illustrated.

Answers to the silhouette figures on p. 53

Numbers 1 to 5 are all the regular owls found in Britain. They are shown in silhouette only, with the typical facial mask in detail.

(1) Tawny or Brown Owl; (2) Barn or Screech Owl; (3) Little Owl; (4) Long-eared Owl; (5) Short-eared Owl

(6) Duck (actually a mallard, but it is the typical duck *shape*)

(7) Partridge (red-legged or common); could also be quail

(8) Pigeon (wood, stock dove, collared or turtle dove)

(9) Skylark (woodlark is stumpier); note long hind toe

(10) Tit (could be either blue or coal)

(11) Wagtail (either pied, grey or yellow)

(12) Thrush (could also be blackbird or ring-ousel)

(13) Warbler (this silhouette would fit chiff-chaff, willow or wood warbler)

(14) Sparrow (could equally be chaffinch or greenfinch; note thick beak)

(15) Woodpecker (pied, barred, or possibly green if very large size)

(16) Nuthatch; (17) Tree-creeper (These can *only* be the birds named)

(18) Spotted Flycatcher (note the upright stance)

(19) Swift (unmistakable and *not* related to swallow family)

(20) Swallow (long streamers on tail identify, except in fledgelings)

(21) House martin (shorter wings, 'fish' tail *white rump* : or sand martin)

(22) Rook (note long, pointed, whitish bill; only 'crow' to wear 'plus-fours')

(23) Carrion crow (heavy *black* bill; usually a solitary species)

(24) Carrion crow flying (but hooded crow or jackdaw would do)

(25) Gull (any of the six regular species could be correct; typical gull shape)

(26) Kestrel (note long, *pointed* wings)

(27) Duck rising (could be almost any species)

(28) Sparrow hawk (note *rounded* wings; does not hover like kestrel)

Index

Note: This index has been made as simple as possible for quick reference, and the birds are indexed under their important characteristics, *viz.* status, field description, illustrations, songs etc. They are frequently mentioned by name in the text of Chapters 1, 4, 5, 8, 9, 10, 11, 12 and 13. Figures in italic represent photographs between pp. 80–81.